Teacher Leadership Practice in High-Performing Schools

This practical book shares key lessons learned from highly effective, award-winning National Blue Ribbon Schools. *Teacher Leadership Practice in High-Performing Schools* explores the important role teachers have in leading schools, the balance administrators must strike between providing teachers with support and trusting them as professionals, and the ways that educators in these schools frequently collaborate across roles and do not operate in isolation. Following vignettes inspired by real schools, each chapter explains and unpacks key lessons learned, situates these lessons within the literature, offers readers robust tools to apply these lessons in their own schools, and includes questions designed to encourage reflection on school practices. This exciting new book helps schools, leadership teams, and individual educators reflect on teacher leadership practice in their schools and determine concrete next steps to increase and improve the impact of teacher leadership.

Jeremy D. Visone is Associate Professor of Educational Leadership and Instructional Technology at Central Connecticut State University, USA. He is a former principal of a National Blue Ribbon School.

Also Available from Routledge Eye on Education
(www.routledge.com/eyeoneducation)

Coaching Education Leaders: A Culturally Responsive Approach to Transforming Schools and Systems
Nancy B. Gutierrez, Michelle Jarney, and Michael Kim

Finding Your Path as a Woman in School Leadership: A Guide for Educators, Allies, and Advocates
Kim Cofino and Christina Botbyl

Empowering Teacher Leadership: Strategies and Systems to Realize Your School's Potential
Jeremy D. Visone

Finding Your Leadership Edge: Balancing Assertiveness and Compassion in Schools
Brad Johnson and Jeremy Johnson

Building Dynamic Teamwork in Schools: 12 Principles of the V Formation to Transform Culture
Brad Johnson and Robert Hinchliffe

Improving Teacher Morale and Motivation: Leadership Strategies That Build Student Success
Ronald Williamson and Barbara R. Blackburn

A Leadership Playbook for Addressing Rapid Change in Education: Empowered for Success
Teresa L. San Martín

Improving Teacher Morale and Motivation: Leadership Strategies that Build Student Success
Ronald Williamson and Barbara R. Blackburn

Lead with Truth: How to Make a Difference in Your School, Your Life, and the Lives of Your Students
Qiana O'Leary

Leading School Culture through Teacher Voice and Agency
Sally J. Zepeda, Philip D. Lanoue, David R. Shafer, and Grant M. Rivera

The Confident School Leader: 7 Keys to Influence and Implement Change
Kara Knight

The Influential School Leader: Inspiring Teachers, Students, and Families Through Social and Organizational Psychology
Craig Murphy and John D'Auria

Teacher Leadership Practice in High-Performing Schools

A Blueprint for Excellence

Jeremy D. Visone

Routledge
Taylor & Francis Group
NEW YORK AND LONDON

Designed cover image: © Getty Images

First published 2025
by Routledge
605 Third Avenue, New York, NY 10158

and by Routledge
4 Park Square, Milton Park, Abingdon, Oxon, OX14 4RN

Routledge is an imprint of the Taylor & Francis Group, an informa business

© 2025 Jeremy D. Visone

The right of Jeremy D. Visone to be identified as author of this work has been asserted in accordance with sections 77 and 78 of the Copyright, Designs and Patents Act 1988.

All rights reserved. The purchase of this copyright material confers the right on the purchasing institution to photocopy or download pages which bear the support material icon and a copyright line at the bottom of the page. No other parts of this book may be reprinted or reproduced or utilised in any form or by any electronic, mechanical, or other means, now known or hereafter invented, including photocopying and recording, or in any information storage or retrieval system, without permission in writing from the publishers.

Trademark notice: Product or corporate names may be trademarks or registered trademarks, and are used only for identification and explanation without intent to infringe.

ISBN: 9781032761558 (hbk)
ISBN: 9781032762289 (pbk)
ISBN: 9781003477310 (ebk)

DOI: 10.4324/9781003477310

Typeset in Optima
by Newgen Publishing UK

Access the Support Material: www.routledge.com/9781032762289

To the school communities of Anna Reynolds and John Wallace, two nationally recognized schools, where I learned how to teach and lead …

Contents

Figures	ix
Tables	x
Meet the Author	xii
Preface	xiii
Acknowledgments	xvii
Acronyms	xviii
Online Support Material	xix

1	**Who Are These Schools, and Why Should I Care?**	1
	Snapshots of Schools at Their Best	3
	Snapshots of Whom, Exactly?	3
	Why Study These Schools?	6
	Key Lessons about Teacher Leadership Practice	7
	Answering Your (Anticipated and Maybe Dismissive) Questions about National Blue Ribbon Schools	10
	Reflect Like a National Blue Ribbon School	14
	Summary	16
	Questions to Consider for Chapter 1	17
2	**Supporting Teacher Leadership for Excellence**	21
	Supportive Culture for Teacher Leadership	23
	Summary	47
	Questions to Consider for Chapter 2	48

Contents

3	**Stepping Up to Get Stuff Done**	**51**
	How Teacher Leadership Manifests	53
	How Do Teachers Lead in Our School?	65
	Summary	67
	Questions to Consider for Chapter 3	69
4	**Supported Autonomy: An Empowering Balance for Teachers' Practice**	**73**
	Who's the Boss of Us?	78
	Autonomy for Teachers, as Considered by Others	81
	Strategic Structures for Excellence	83
	Back to Trust Again	84
	How Supported and/or Autonomous Are Our Teachers?	85
	Summary	100
	Questions to Consider for Chapter 4	102
5	**Collaborative Professionalism for Teams' Work**	**106**
	The Traditional Challenge for Schools: The School as an Archipelago	109
	Collective Work to the Rescue!	112
	Helping Our Staff "See in Systems"	117
	Is Our School an Archipelago?	140
	Summary	143
	Questions to Consider for Chapter 5	145

Glossary	148

Figures

Figures and tables with the support material icon are available as downloadable and editable documents in the Support Material collection for this book (see Online Support Material page).

2.1	Supportive conditions for teacher leadership	24
3.1	Four main categories of teacher leadership found in National Blue Ribbon Schools	54
3.2	Ways teachers manifested instructional leadership in National Blue Ribbon Schools	55
3.3	Guiding questions about teachers as decision-makers	60
4.1	Meeting content versus teacher autonomy quadrant diagram	86
4.2	Instructional support versus teacher autonomy quadrant diagram	91
5.1	Free body diagram for systems thinking tool	124
5.2	Sample free body diagram about math intervention system	126
5.3	Sample system improvement tool about rigorous coursework process	135

Tables

1.1	The three key lessons about teacher leadership practice in National Blue Ribbon Schools	8
1.2	Prompts from the 2022 National Blue Ribbon Schools Program application	15
2.1	The first key lesson about teacher leadership practice in National Blue Ribbon Schools	23
2.2	Actions and messages that espouse a teacher leadership expectation	26
2.3	Teacher leadership self-assessment tool for schools	28
2.4	Leadership team analysis tool	42
2.5	The Five Facets of Trust, as applied to teacher leadership work	46
3.1	The first key lesson (again) about teacher leadership practice in National Blue Ribbon Schools	53
3.2	Professional learning audit tool for teacher leadership	58
3.3	Teacher leader innovation efforts inventory	62
3.4	Teacher leader talents and interests inventory	66
4.1	The second key lesson about teacher leadership practice in National Blue Ribbon Schools	77
4.2	Supported autonomy self-assessment tool for schools	93

Tables

5.1	The third key lesson about teacher leadership practice in National Blue Ribbon Schools	109
5.2	System improvement tool	128
5.3	System updates tool	137
5.4	Sample system updates tool about common planning time	138
5.5	Is our school an archipelago? Questionnaire	140

Meet the Author

Jeremy D. Visone is a faculty member in the Department of Educational Leadership & Instructional Technology at Central Connecticut State University (CCSU), where, in addition to teaching graduate students who are aspiring educational leaders, he also serves as chair of the University Institutional Review Board, which oversees all research with human subjects on campus. His research interests include teacher leadership, collaborative structures for teachers, teacher evaluation, the development of problem-solving skills for aspiring educational leaders, and the practices of U.S. National Blue Ribbon Schools. Jeremy is also the author of *Empowering Teacher Leadership: Strategies and Systems to Realize Your School's Potential* (2022, Routledge). Prior to his work at CCSU, Jeremy was a building leader at the elementary and secondary levels, most recently serving as the proud principal of Anna Reynolds Elementary School in Newington, CT, U.S.A., which was named a U.S. National Blue Ribbon School in 2016.

When not focusing on teaching and research, Jeremy can be found at the gym or outside, finding ways to be active. Jeremy lives in Cromwell, Connecticut, U.S.A., with his wife, Kerry, and their three preteen and teenage children, which tells you all you need to know.

Jeremy enjoys connecting with readers of his works. Be encouraged to contact him to share your connections to ideas in this book.

Preface

In November 2016, I had the great pleasure to travel to Washington, D.C., for the annual U.S. National Blue Ribbon School awards celebration. This invitation-only event featured hundreds of superintendents, principals, and teachers from across the United States, who had in common that their schools were recognized by their respective states for either their overall exemplary student outcomes or exemplary achievement gap-closing efforts. In either case, these schools were being recognized by the U.S. Department of Education due to their students' success and because this success was noteworthy in relation to other schools in their respective states.

I was invited because I was principal at Anna Reynolds Elementary School through 2016, when it was recognized with this distinction, due to our dedication and skill, and our students' subsequent success. It was a tremendous honor to attend, from the networking with like-minded individuals from across the country to hearing from inspirational speakers, such as then-Secretary of Education John King Jr. Our small delegation of proud administrators and a teacher made the most of our visit to the nation's capital, visiting meaningful landmarks, museums, and sights. However, for me, the trip was meaningful on another level.

Whenever I attended any events associated with the celebration, which is more like a multiple-day conference, I was struck by the potential in the room. Within the confines of this conference, among all these administrators and teachers from high-performing schools, so many great ideas and practices surely existed. If only someone could capture and share them …

Preface

That someone, it turns out, would be *me*—at least in part. That same year, 2016, I made the very difficult, but ultimately rewarding, decision to leave Anna Reynolds and begin work as a full-time faculty member of educational leadership at Central Connecticut State University. From this new vantage point within the profession, I have spent the last eight years researching the practices of National Blue Ribbon Schools, reading through a random sampling of these schools' (60, to be exact) applications to the program and talking to their principals and teacher leaders. The findings have been both inspiring and reassuring to me. For inspiration, I heard about teachers going above and beyond during the COVID-19 pandemic, stepping up to do what was needed in their schools and communities. Examples included supporting colleagues with integration of technology, providing their fellow teachers with morale boosts, and serving meals to their students' families when schools were not operating in person. For reassurance, I learned that what made these schools noteworthy, overall, was nothing so grandiose or complicated that other schools could not learn from or even replicate their practices. Rather, these schools displayed identifiable and replicable patterns of practice that I will outline in this book.

The patterns I found included very intentional practices to encourage, expect, and celebrate teacher leadership; teacher leadership practice across many aspects of school life, such as teaching and learning, operations, innovation of practice, and extension beyond the school; a form of autonomy that was balanced by robust support from administrators and colleagues; and collaboration that resembled what literature informs us is healthy and effective practice.

The result of these eight years of study is a work that combines research about teacher leadership, collaboration, systems thinking, and other relevant aspects of our profession; my specific findings from National Blue Ribbon Schools; and a variety of reflective tools and other figures designed to provide you and your school's team the opportunity either to affirm what you have established or move toward practices that are informed by these schools' successes. Similar to my classes for future educational leaders, this book will help you move from theory to practice.

This work is segmented into five chapters, which are themed around explaining the National Blue Ribbon Schools Program and building a case for examining the recognized schools' practices, foundations for teacher leadership, manifestations of teacher leadership practice, the balance between autonomy and support for teachers, and collaborative practice considerations. Each chapter begins with an instructive vignette. Though the vignettes include pseudonyms, the situations are real, and they help readers concretely visualize the content that will follow in the chapters, whether vignettes present examples of effective practice, "non-examples" of effective practice, or something in between. Chapters also consistently reference both my research findings from National Blue Ribbon Schools as well as connections to literature and other research, both within education and other professional fields. Further, each chapter contains tools that readers can use to reflect upon their own schools' practices and move them forward, considering findings from my National Blue Ribbon Schools' research. There is also a summary at the conclusion of each chapter. Finally, chapters conclude with a series of questions to deepen readers' reflection and learning.

I shared a perspective in my last book, *Empowering Teacher Leadership: Strategies and Systems to Realize Your School's Potential* (Visone, 2022, Routledge), that is relevant here as well. Namely, in our profession, we hear often about a model of teaching or leadership that is touted by someone we respect as *the pathway* to success. In my experience, the contextualized nature of individual communities and schools renders this "one-size-fits-all" approach inadequate. Further, I would never imply that what I share is the only route to success. Rather, I prefer to share what I have learned from others—both from the literature and via my own research with schools—so that you, the discerning reader, can make informed decisions about what you will try to implement in your own setting. This is more a recipe book, with many excellent dishes to try, than it is a step-by-step manual to put together that complicated piece of furniture.

This book is designed for school leaders of all types. Obviously, administrators will benefit from connections to research and concrete means to move their schools forward. Teachers and other non-administrative educators who serve on their schools' leadership teams can assist their administrators in the work of school improvement. In addition, teacher leaders in many varying roles, both formal and informal, will benefit from this work. They will be affirmed to know that many of their own practices are considered leadership, and they will be inspired by teacher leadership efforts within National Blue Ribbon Schools. Further, through the tools and reflective materials, teacher leaders (or those aspiring to be teacher leaders) will learn ways to further express their leadership and help their schools move toward greatness.

I enjoyed conducting this research, and I hope that you find the results interesting and informative. Perhaps, with some reflection and strategic implementation of what I have suggested herein, your school might next be recognized as standing out among its peers!

Let's get to work!

Acknowledgments

The author would like to extend special thanks to Dr. Renée A. Savoie, of the Connecticut State Department of Education; Ashley Frame, of the New Hampshire Department of Education; and other State Department of Education officials, who wished to remain anonymous, for their time and invaluable insights into the selection process for National Blue Ribbon Schools. This work is so much stronger, thanks to your expertise and "insider" perspectives.

Further, the author would like to thank the many principals and teacher leaders in recognized National Blue Ribbon Schools who agreed to be interviewed. Thank you for sharing your insights, successes, and struggles, as well as for your dedicated work with students. Ultimately, this book is your collective story.

Acronyms

ASCD   Association for Supervision and Curriculum Development (now known simply as ASCD)
COVID-19   coronavirus disease 2019
ELA   English language arts
NBRS   National Blue Ribbon Schools
NGSS   Next Generation Science Standards
OECD   Organisation for Economic Cooperation and Development
PTO   parent teacher organization
SG   shared governance
SPED   special education

Online Support Material

Some of the resources in this book can be accessed online by visiting this book's product page on our website: www.routledge.com/9781032762289 (then follow the links indicating Support Material, which you can then download directly).

- **Figure 5.1** Free body diagram for systems thinking tool
- **Table 1.2** Prompts from the 2022 National Blue Ribbon Schools Program application
- **Table 2.3** Teacher leadership self-assessment tool for schools
- **Table 2.4** Leadership team analysis tool
- **Table 3.2** Professional learning audit tool for teacher leadership
- **Table 3.3** Teacher leader innovation efforts inventory
- **Table 3.4** Teacher leader talents and interests inventory
- **Table 4.2** Supported autonomy self-assessment tool for schools
- **Table 5.2** System improvement tool
- **Table 5.3** System updates tool
- **Table 5.5** Is our school an archipelago? Questionnaire

Who Are These Schools, and Why Should I Care?

As principal of Evergreen Point Elementary School,[1] your day is progressing as many typically do—*too many tasks and not enough time*. On this cold, February Monday morning, you had raced over to your district's central office for an elementary principals' meeting, leaving behind loose ends related to substitute coverage (thank goodness for your efficient and independent administrative assistant!), several behavioral investigations, and numerous teachers' requests for a few minutes of your time. Returning to the school near lunchtime, with your head spinning from a list of action items that emanated from the meeting, you receive a note from your administrative assistant, Tammy, that you missed a call from a person named "Jeff" from the state department of education. Having had no recent contact with the state department of education, your mind races to determine what this call might concern. Naturally, like any school leader, your thoughts lean toward some of the worst possible scenarios. *Is our school being investigated for something? Did we err on one of our schoolwide data-collection reports?*

You head into your office and quietly close the door. With your blank pad of paper next to you and pen in hand, you dial Jeff's phone number, expecting to document the negative news that is surely coming. After a quick exchange of pleasantries, Jeff gets at his purpose:

"Have you seen your school's Smarter Balanced [the state-adopted standardized test for reading and mathematics] results?"

"Of course! We examine those as soon as they are made available every summer. We shared them with staff as the year began, and we have set goals, accordingly. Why?" Jeff's question seemed an odd one, and this had done nothing to alleviate your initial concerns about the call. And then ...

"Because they are great!" Jeff indicated. "And your overall accountability index—you know, that's test scores, chronic absenteeism rate, physical fitness, and more—was off the charts!"

"Oh, well, *thanks* ... our students and teachers have been working hard. What's this about?" Enough with the dancing around the purpose, as you still figured this was buttering you up for the other shoe to drop.

"Your school's index was not just great, but it was one of the best in the state. Your school [sidebar: a Title I school with average resources that routinely ranked *third or fourth* [out of four!] *among the district's elementary schools* on nearly every measure when you arrived to start your tenure at the school] beat out the likes of schools in Oak Hill, Rocky Point, and Pine Valley [sidebar, again: districts that have incredible community wealth and allegedly finance 'world class' public schools]."

"Wow ... I was not expecting to hear that. Awesome!"

"Yeah, you should be very proud of yourselves. Congratulations on this accomplishment, but I also want you to know that, because of this excellent performance, *your school is being nominated by our office for the National Blue Ribbon Schools Program*. After this call, I will be sending you directions and an application that you will need to complete for the U.S. Department of Education by the beginning of April. You just need to work with your staff to complete the application, continue what you are doing, and if your performance is high again for the data from this coming spring, your school will be recognized. Then you will go and meet the president!"

"Uh—Wait ... *what!?*" Wow. This was a lot to process, though it was generally welcome news. Certainly, this information was infinitely better than what you had thought you would be discussing. And then, Jeff added the clincher that really threw you for a loop ...

"So, what have you been doing over there?"

This question causes you to pause. *What is it, exactly, that we do here at Evergreen Point that led to this success and recognition?*

Snapshots of Schools at Their Best

Teachers, administrators, related service providers, paraeducators, and all other staff members have important roles to play in the successful working of a school. In my writing and work with students who are aspiring educational leaders, I advocate for an understanding of systems to help schools improve what they do. As such, schools should examine roles, contributions, communications channels, protocols, team structures, schedules, forums for discussion, alliances, agreements, beliefs, and all other means through which their work—the provision of an excellent and equitable education for all students, in case you were wondering—is transacted. When a school produces results manifesting that systems within are operating at a high level of effectiveness, and children are being served in an exemplary manner, we would be foolish not to ask ourselves, *what exactly are they doing over there to contribute to their success?* More importantly, we should follow with: *what are they doing **that we are not**?* This book offers precisely such an opportunity. You will "peek inside" to examine the inner workings (specifically, teacher practices, focusing on teacher leadership) within high-performing schools at their most effective moments—the snapshots when we should be examining their practices to answer the two aforementioned questions. Of course, you are a busy educator, and you do not have the time to determine which schools are worthy of study (i.e., those schools that are experiencing a run of success which warrants your attention), let alone *actually study* these schools, which are spread all over the United States! If you have good intuition about such things, you may have correctly predicted that sharing lessons about what teacher leadership practice looks like at these schools is the very purpose of this book. I have the time to study these schools so that you don't have to!

Let's find out who these schools are and why we want to study them.

Snapshots of Whom, Exactly?

My work to locate schools performing at high levels of effectiveness is made infinitely easier by a recognition system that has operated for decades in the United States. Namely, the National Blue Ribbon Schools (NBRS) Program is operated by the U.S. Department of

Education. For more than 40 years, since 1982, the NBRS Program has annually recognized hundreds of public and nonpublic schools that represent one of two categories: exemplary high performing and exemplary achievement gap closing. In the former case, these schools have demonstrated top 15% performance in both English language arts and mathematics in their respective states. For the latter category of schools, they have demonstrated growth in terms of subgroup achievement gaps (i.e., racial identity, exceptionality status, socioeconomic background, etc.) that distinguishes them from other schools in their state. At least one-third of each state's nominated schools must have a high proportion of students (defined as at least 40%) identified as being from disadvantaged backgrounds, such as students who are from lower socioeconomic backgrounds, who qualify for special education with an identified exceptionality, or who qualify for English language services, and so on (U.S. Department of Education, n.d.-b). States can define what "disadvantaged backgrounds" means in their contexts.

I spoke with officials in several states about their process for selecting NBRS. The process varies across states, but there are some commonalities. All states select schools in the exemplary high-performing category. At least 12 states, as of 2022, select schools in the exemplary gap-closing category, and even more states are working to upgrade their data systems to begin selecting schools in this latter category, as well. Whether exemplary high-performing or exemplary gap-closing, measures of success can include a multitude of variables beyond standardized test scores, including attendance; graduation rates; access to the arts; college and career readiness; physical fitness; performance of high-needs students (i.e., students with exceptionalities, multilingual learners, and those who qualify for free and reduced lunch, etc.); access to rigorous coursework; performance versus cohorts of similar students; consistency of achievement over time; and more. Thus, states are recognizing schools that meet the needs of the *whole child*, as opposed to a strictly academic focus. Further, given that these schools typically appear on a ranked list of many high-performing or gap-closing schools, states also look beyond typical data points to examine such less quantifiable attributes as family and community engagement and other community stories of interest. States aim to highlight schools that have succeeded and have noteworthy accomplishments that may not have been previously recognized. In other words, the program recognizes schools beyond just those with ample available resources.

For context, in 2021, the NBRS Program recognized 325 schools across 45 states, with the vast majority (302) being public schools. Public schools have been the focus of my research, since they offer the fairest comparisons; these schools must operate within more defined parameters for accountability, testing, licensing/hiring, and the students they are obligated to serve. Within the 302 recognized public schools in 2021, nearly half, or 47%, met the 40% threshold for students identified as disadvantaged. About 69% of the schools were elementary, while 15% each were at the middle and high school levels. The final 1% consisted of PreK-12 schools. In terms of setting, 44% of the schools were in suburban areas, while 34% were identified as operating in rural or small towns or cities, leaving 22% of schools in urban areas. Almost half (46%) of the schools were Title I schools, which is an indication of school economic need, relative to other schools in their districts, and only 11% of the schools were schools of choice, leaving 89% of the schools as those that serviced children in their own communities (U.S. Department of Education, n.d.-a).

In 2022, the story was similar, with 297 recognized schools in 45 states and 273 public schools. Of the 273 recognized public schools in 2022, an identical 47% met the 40% threshold for students identified as disadvantaged when compared with 2021. About 71% of the schools were elementary, while 11% were at the middle level and 15% were at the high school level. The final 3% consisted of PreK-12 schools. In terms of setting, 47% of the schools were in suburban areas, while 37% were identified as operating in rural or small towns or cities, leaving 16% of schools in urban areas. Again, almost half (49%) of the schools were Title I schools, and only 10% of the schools were schools of choice, leaving 90% of the schools as those that serviced children in their own communities (U.S. Department of Education, n.d.-a). These NBRS were spread over every different U.S. context and represented many schools that are far from the most privileged schools in the economically "cushiest" (not a scientific term, but an appropriate description here) settings. They are the schools next door, so to speak.

Historically, the NBRS Program has been seen as a source of information for the profession about a variety of important school functions: principals' practices, school culture transformation, reading strategies, mission statements, character education, teacher leadership, teacher collaboration, and overall practices (McKinney et al., 2015; National Association of Elementary School Principals, 1994, 1998; Perfetto et al., 2013; Visone, 2018, 2022, 2023, 2024). In other words, these schools have much to offer the field! Further, the NBRS Program itself has examined the applications of schools to the program to share insights into these schools' success. In the years 2016 and 2018, the U.S. Department of Education (n.d.-c) identified four key drivers of these schools' success, as identified by the schools themselves. These drivers were student supports, instruction, structural school supports, and curricula. As a professional educator, it is likely that none of these identified drivers of success come as a surprise to you. After all, the main work of schools is to support student success through effective instruction and meaningful curricula. However, these categories of success are just that—categories within which greater meaning can be identified.

The research findings outlined in this book will help unpack broad categories of teacher leadership practice. I have had the pleasure of studying NBRS since 2016, and research with randomly selected NBRS that were recognized in 2016, 2019, 2020, and 2021 informed this work. I have studied more than 60 of these schools, which represent all types of contexts in the United States—urban, rural, suburban, all regions of the country, large schools, small schools, elementary schools, secondary schools, high percentages of students with needs, and so on. Data sources consisted of interviews with principals and teacher leaders, as well as schools' collaboratively developed applications to the program. In this book, I will share patterns of teacher leadership practice observed across these schools.

Why Study These Schools?

It is logical to wonder why busy teachers and administrators should concern themselves with what is happening in other schools. You might be thinking: *we have enough going on right in front of us!* However, dedicating a bit of time to expand beyond our own narrow fields of professional vision can bring new ideas and energy into our, sometimes, stagnant school settings. To gather new insights, it is common for American educators to examine the work of schools in other countries where student outcomes are consistently higher. For example, we often examine practices in Canada (Campbell, 2017), Finland (Sahlberg, 2021; Sahlberg & Walker, 2021), or Singapore (Teacher Leadership Exploratory Consortium, 2012) and ask what leads to these countries' students being such strong performers on international tests. For starters, a common element found across these international studies was the presence of teacher leadership, which, intuitively, has also been a consistent finding across my study of NBRS.

There are also other systems of recognition for schools globally. For example, T4 Education, a U.K.-based organization that seeks to bring together educators from around the world in a global network of collaboration and sharing for the improvement of student learning and community advancement, recently announced their inaugural "World's Best School Prizes" to five schools in Scotland, Uganda, Chile, Philippines, and the United States (T4 Education, 2022). The prizes were awarded in five separate categories, which included community collaboration, environmental action, innovation, overcoming adversity, and supporting healthy lives. These aims are as valuable as any found in the accountability systems for NBRS, and I would argue that these schools are as worthy of study as those in this work. There are lessons to be learned from successful schools that are measured in varied ways.

However, circling back to our purpose, these NBRS offer some unique reasons to attract our interest. First, as stated above, these schools have proven over a period of several school years that they deliver on the most basic of purposes for their students—that students can learn. Also, these schools have seen relative success within the specific contexts of their own states, and, again, there is the requirement that at least one-third of recognized schools have significant numbers (at least 40%) of students from disadvantaged backgrounds, meaning that these schools are finding success, despite barriers that are often used to excuse low performance. Finally, at the precise moment when these schools are seeing arguably their greatest successes, they are asked to reflect on what exactly they do to achieve their outstanding results. The schools' introspection and analysis provide a veritable goldmine of practices for us to examine.

Key Lessons about Teacher Leadership Practice

Throughout this book, we will examine key lessons about teacher leadership practice learned from these effective schools. These key lessons from NBRS are outlined in Table 1.1. It is likely that you are not surprised by anything on this list. From my perspective, this is a positive

Table 1.1 The three key lessons about teacher leadership practice in National Blue Ribbon Schools

teacher leadership	Leadership at our school is not limited to individuals with formal titles. Teachers are valued and supported as leaders, and they step up to do what is needed for our collective success.
supported autonomy	Teachers at our school are provided the supports they need to effectively educate students. However, teachers are trusted by leaders to determine how to best meet students' needs.
collaborative ethos and systems	Educators across roles, particularly teachers, do not work in isolation. Educators at our school learn, solve problems, plan, and innovate collaboratively.

development. After all, this means that there are no magic secrets at work in these schools; no unattainable, clandestine practices; no ideas so revolutionary that your school or district could never replicate them. Rather, the key lessons demonstrate that these schools have found success via the very practices that you likely want of your own schools, such as building a foundation of solid professional relationships, creating systems for teacher empowerment and collaboration, and allowing teachers to spend their time focusing on their most important work—*teaching students*! Hopefully, this "revelation of non-revelation" is a relief to you; it certainly was to me as I researched the schools' practices. I will briefly summarize the lessons next, and each lesson will be expounded upon in greater detail in the subsequent chapters.

The first lesson (see Chapters 2 and 3) encompasses *teacher leadership* itself. The ability for teachers to exhibit leadership starts with a solid, supportive culture built on professional relationships. Some of you are lucky enough to work in a school with a positive school culture, where work does not feel like work because you truly enjoy what you do and those with whom you do it. Others dread going to work every day because of a toxic, energy-sucking, productivity- (and *soul*-!) crushing climate where leadership is lacking. Still others are somewhere in the middle of these two extremes. NBRS offer ideas to help move all schools toward the first type of culture.

Typically, effective schools ground their positive culture in trusting relationships among stakeholders (Tschannen-Moran & Gareis, 2015; Tschannen-Moran, 2001). We also know that this trust can lead to feelings of safety; cooperation with leadership; and, not surprisingly, better collaboration and greater effort exerted (Sinek, 2014), two prerequisites of effective teacher leadership. The studied schools generally have just this type of foundational culture that is positive and supportive, allowing teacher leadership to take root and add value.

These schools get things done because administrators and teachers work together. Much research supports the concept of distributed leadership (Diamond & Spillane, 2016; Leithwood et al., 2007; Nerlino, 2020). Now, more than ever, in our COVID-19-influenced educational system, we need to rely on teachers, who are in the figurative trenches, contending with realities not experienced by many of their administrators when they were teachers, to contribute their ideas and perspectives to the leadership of schools. Teachers have front-row seats to mental health challenges, social and emotional learning needs, and inequities, and this unique vantage point renders their insights of critical importance. Further, formal school leaders (i.e., principals, assistant principals, etc.) cannot effectively perform all the leadership work of their schools by themselves; the work of leading schools is much too complex and voluminous to leave for just a few, formal leaders (Danielson, 2007; Nerlino, 2020). Finally, schools in other successful countries trust their teachers' decision-making and hold teachers, professionally and societally, in high esteem (Sahlberg & Walker, 2021). In the studied NBRS, there was ample and healthy teacher leadership practice, ranging from formal decision-making forums led and populated by teachers to informal examples of teachers "stepping up" to do what needed to be done.

Continuing with the theme of trusting teachers, a pattern found across so many of these NBRS was *supported autonomy* (see Chapter 4). To perform their jobs well, teachers need both support and agency. Support comes from formal leaders and colleagues, and can include tangible resources, like professional learning, curricula, time to plan, materials, and systems for collaboration and student intervention. Agency emanates from autonomy for teachers, where they are trusted as professionals to make decisions, such as those they make in the classroom each day and those they make when working collaboratively with colleagues. Analogously, great thinkers in educational leadership have noted the relationship in highly effective school districts between tight control over what should be taught and what will be monitored, and less rigid control over how individual schools and teachers implement an instructional program (Elmore, 2000; Fullan, 2007; Marzano, 2003; Murphy & Hallinger, 1988). In the case of NBRS, a healthy balance between tighter control over the "what" and less-rigid control over the "how" was evident within schools at the teachers' level. Teachers were provided with resources and structures and direction, and yet, they were allowed to innovate, create, and collaborate among themselves to take it from there.

The final key lesson from the studied schools is about how teachers work together (see Chapter 5). In short, they worked collaboratively, viewing their professional interactions as integral to their success. One of the great challenges of education, traditionally, has been its isolation of teachers and its resulting lack of instructional consistency—what the late, great educational thinker Richard Elmore (2005) referred to as a problem of "scale." Isolation of teachers from their colleagues (whether structurally or voluntarily) has recently been shown, not surprisingly, to be negatively correlated with student outcomes (Krakehl et al., 2020). Teacher learning is best when it is, among other factors, collaborative (Croft et al., 2010; Learning Forward, n.d., 2019; Wei et al., 2010). Teachers at the studied NBRS worked within coordinated systems designed for their collaboration, and they displayed collaborative learning, mindsets, and behaviors.

The three key lessons about teacher practice in NBRS will be outlined in greater detail, complete with means to apply these lessons to your own school settings, in the remaining four chapters.

Answering Your (Anticipated and Maybe Dismissive) Questions about National Blue Ribbon Schools

If you are an educator in the United States, it is possible that you can identify schools in your midst that have been recognized in this manner. However, many teachers and leaders in U.S. schools do not have a solid understanding of this program and why its recognized schools can serve as a resource for those looking to improve practice in their own schools. Thus,

I will dedicate space here to addressing some questions about the program and the utility of collectively examining these schools' experiences via some "*But, Jeremy, …?*" questions and/or comments.

But … these schools have all the advantages and are predisposed to success, right? First, recall that NBRS are selected by student outcomes defined in two different ways. There are those with high overall performance, and there are schools that have made exemplary progress over the course of time in closing achievement gaps for subgroups of students. For the latter group, recognition means that these schools have overcome some significant challenges related to student outcomes, meaning they started in a not-so-desirable place (Read: *not high performance for subgroups or overall*) and have worked their way out of that position.

Additionally, recall that there is a requirement that each state ensures that at least one-third of nominated schools have at least 40% of their students from disadvantaged backgrounds (i.e., students who qualify for free and reduced lunch, special education services, and English language services, for example), meaning these schools have significant student needs to address. Finally, by accepting schools from nearly every state and other jurisdictions (i.e., Washington, D.C., Puerto Rico, Department of Defense, etc.), the schools represent the diversity of states' (and other budgetary entities') school funding support. Perhaps most importantly, according to those who lead the selection of NBRS, state NBRS Program Liaisons, who are often state department of education staff members, sometimes working in their states' accountability divisions, states are specifically seeking to showcase schools that represent their states' diversity and character. Simply, NBRS Program Liaisons and their colleagues do not want to choose schools that have the largest budgets and the least community need, thereby selecting schools that are predestined (on paper) for success. NBRS are nominated because of (a) their aforementioned success and, often, (b) their lack of conformity to the "schools of privilege" stereotype. In addition to the quantification of student outcomes across the many categories of success, there is also an "art" to the nomination process, whereby states attempt to tell positive stories about schools that have succeeded, despite obstacles. Thus, by definition and via practice, NBRS include among them many schools that are far from having all the advantages.

But … these schools are looking for the recognition and will do and say anything, right? NBRS typically do not seek recognition, at all. States identify the schools behind-the-scenes and alert their principals to the nomination, like in this chapter's opening vignette. It is only *after nomination by their states* that schools complete the application to the program and continue to, hopefully, produce the patterns of success that will corroborate their candidacy the following fall, when final decisions and announcements are made.

As far as schools being compelled to say anything, one can certainly make a reasonable argument that human nature will lead principals and teachers to present their schools in the best possible light. I will not dispute this general line of thinking. However, recall that these schools produce results that suggest that they have some practices worthy of our attention, so we should be appreciative that they will share what has worked for them! Further, these schools' teachers and principals were not shy about sharing with me practices at their own, celebrated schools that were *not* ideal. I share about some of these situations, which were outliers within the dataset, in subsequent chapters. These "nonexamples," as I like to call them, can be instructive, as well.

But ... these schools are not like our schools! That stuff would never work in my context. Since I do not actually know *your* school, this is a really difficult argument to rebut. However, I will, again, point to the diverse nature of the settings, contexts, and demographic makeups of the various schools in this pool of NBRS. The pool is vast and diverse. There are likely myriad similarities between your school and many schools recognized by the program. I will concede that it is wise to always consider your own specific school context to determine what lessons from NBRS are most applicable to your school's present reality. Perhaps, you just need a tweak or two to your systems to accelerate your success. In other cases, toxic cultures or ineffective systems might indicate that many, if not most, of the lessons will directly apply to your school. Keep in mind that adopting practices, tomorrow, is often not enough to yield immediate improvements, as we know that deep, meaningful change in schools takes years to accomplish (Wallace Foundation, 2013). You might be right that some of what you will read will not work in your school—*tomorrow*—but that does not mean it cannot work in your school over the long term. For example, building a strong foundation of trusting relationships among professionals is longitudinal work. Start small with the relationships you can control, and over time, the culture will benefit.

But ... are you saying these schools are perfect, and we should just do whatever they do?

Nope.

These schools are not perfect, and, as noted above, principals and teachers told me as much. However, they have found ways to overcome their lack of perfection to produce some impressive results relative to peer institutions in their states. With respect to doing what these NBRS do, you need to understand your context deeply, in part to determine what lessons from this research can help you move forward toward a better future for your students. I would never advocate for a blind and full adoption of *any* advice *anyone* provides about how to improve outcomes for your students at your school. However, these findings were patterns across schools, so there is power due to the findings' consistency across the sample. Further, I challenge you to find a lesson in this book that is not worthy of serious consideration and does not represent best practice in our profession. In my humble opinion, you will find the ideas herein relatable and actionable and the reflection tools applicable to nearly any school setting.

But … these schools just got lucky! It should be noted that, frequently, schools are tracked for years prior to their nomination. Thus, they have shown a consistent pattern of success over time, and their recognition is not the result of a fluke or good fortune. Rather, consistently solid performance and/or improvement has led to recognition.

But … why not look to other countries that have had more recent, consistent success than the United States? We should! We will agree to agree here. As a career educator, I take the perspective that any situation or dataset can be a learning opportunity. Studying schools in Finland, Canada, and Singapore, among others, is a worthy and meaningful venture. After all, at times, those within a closed system tend to view things in myopic ways. It is great to see outside your own system to acquire fresh and different perspectives. But … it is equally as important to find out where schools are seeing success *within* our system. These schools are, essentially, playing by the same rules as we are (i.e., accountability, funding, licensure, etc.), and, more importantly, they exist within the same context that includes a pluralistic society that has an often-negative perception of public education and many competing interests that exert pressure on our schools. It is within *this* context that NBRS have found their recent success. Let's leverage their successes (and likely, previous failures) for our benefit and for the ultimate improvement of outcomes for our own students.

But … this system recognizes only one narrow definition of student performance—standardized tests! This critique might have been fair

10 years ago, but systems for accountability in states have evolved to reflect more expansive definitions of success. States are including variables like graduation rate, physical fitness, access to rigorous courses, attendance, and other metrics that evaluate more of the "whole child." Thus, schools demonstrating high performance now are doing so across a more well-rounded set of markers for their students. They are, in effect, doing *both*; they are succeeding via traditional measures (i.e., standardized tests) and more inclusive metrics. *Win/win!*

Reflect Like a National Blue Ribbon School

So, what if your school has not been recognized as exemplary—*yet?* Your school has dedicated educators, like you (as evidenced by your reading this book!), who are motivated to improve the work of your school, and that is a huge step in the right direction. Another step toward your future school greatness is reflecting on what your school does (and *does not*) do well. It is instructive and helpful to unpack your school's operation in the way that NBRS do when their educators collaborate to complete the program application. These completed applications are publicly available from the U.S. Department of Education (n.d.-a). To save you the trouble of locating an application yourself, I have provided highlights from the open-ended prompts on the 2022 NBRS Program application in Table 1.2. Note that an editable and printable version of this school reflection tool can be found in the Support Material collection for this book.

Take some time to reflect on how your school operates and what makes it unique, effective, and not-so-effective. There is no need to worry about aesthetics in this exercise. Bulleted text and phrases will do. Your purpose is to capture the *what?* and *how?* of your school. Your responses can be useful when comparing your school's practices to the key lessons about teacher leadership practice as they are unpacked in subsequent chapters. To improve what we do, we need to have a firm understanding of where we are now. This task is best completed collaboratively, naturally, so find some friends and/or colleagues, and let the conversation about moving toward greatness begin!

Who Are These Schools, and Why Should I Care?

Table 1.2 Prompts from the 2022 National Blue Ribbon Schools Program application

Available publicly on the U.S. Department of Education (n.d.-a) website.

1. Provide an overall snapshot of your school, including your community, demographic information, historical context, and key strategies used within the school that have encouraged and challenged all students to develop their full potential academically, emotionally, physically, socially, and culturally. Also, describe any creative or innovative techniques/programs the school has implemented. These techniques/programs could be academic, socio-emotional, cultural, or other, but they should be something that sets the school apart and contributes to its unique character.
2. Provide an overall curricular approach which may include overarching philosophy or approaches common across subject areass.
3. For each core academic content area taught in your school, explain how students acquire foundational skills, and describe the effort/progress the school is making to improve the skills of students performing below and above grade level. Then provide highlights of the curricula, instruction, and assessments.
4. For all other content areas, provide highlights of the curricula, instruction, and assessments.
5. For secondary schools only: describe how the curriculum supports college and career readiness.*
5. For schools that offer preschool for three- and/or four-year-old students only: describe: (a) the core curriculum areas provided; (b) the alignment of early childhood and K-Grade 3 academic standards; and (c) any indicators of the impact of early education on school readiness and success in the primary grades.*
6. Describe academic supports for students (a) who are performing below grade level, (b) who are performing above grade level, (c) with exceptionalities/have special needs, (d) who are English Language/Multilingual Learners, and (e) representing other populations of traditional need (i.e., migrant families, unhoused families, etc.).
7. Describe student engagement.
8. Describe family and community engagement.
9. Describe the professional culture.
10. Describe school leadership.
11. Describe culturally responsive teaching and learning.
12. Select and describe the most important practice at your school for academic success.

*Schools will usually only answer one version of Item 5, as only one version typically applies.

Summary

The U.S. Department of Education recognizes hundreds of schools each year through the National Blue Ribbon Schools (NBRS) Program. This program recognizes schools as either (a) exemplary high performing or (b) exemplary achievement gap closing. At least 12 states recognize schools in the latter category. At least one-third of the schools nominated by any state must have at least 40% of their students from disadvantaged backgrounds, often defined as qualifying for free and reduced lunch, special education with an identified exceptionality, and/or English language services. State Program Liaisons have shared processes to select schools, which vary by state. However, states aim to select schools that have important stories to share, overcome significant obstacles, exhibit high participation rates (i.e., they are not "hiding" students with needs from their data), manifest consistently strong results over time, and/or produce high levels of success for all groups of students.

NBRS are a valuable source of practices that have resulted in student success, and they have been studied by various authors and organizations over the past few decades. In the this book, the NBRS studied provided the following key lessons about teacher leadership practice: cultures of support, including strong professional relationships, multidirectional trust, and distributed leadership, underlie teacher leadership; teachers help lead their schools and contribute to their schools' success, beyond their own classrooms, often stepping up to do what is necessary; teachers experience supported autonomy, whereby formal leaders and colleagues provide teachers what they need to be successful, but much decision-making is still left to teams of and individual teachers; and educators collaborate regularly, learning, planning, and innovating together, rather than in isolation. In the subsequent chapters, these key lessons will be unpacked and explored, both with respect to specific findings from my research and how these findings can be applied to other school contexts, including yours.

Questions to Consider for Chapter 1:
Who Are These Schools, and Why Should I Care?

1. Think about schools in your area that have been recognized in the past, whether through the U.S. National Blue Ribbon Schools (NBRS) Program, state accountability programs, or other systems of recognition. Based upon your understanding, what made these schools stand out? From what you know, did these schools do something that yours does not?
2. From the short introduction to the three key lessons about teacher practice in NBRS, how do these principles resonate with what occurs in your school?
3. After completing the *Reflecting Like a National Blue Ribbon School* tool (Table 1.2), how would you describe your school's:
    a. areas of success and celebration?
    b. areas for growth?
    c. unique features, programs, processes, etc.?
    d. foundation for future success?
    e. community assets?
    f. goals for improvement?
4. In anticipation of the coming chapters, what do you hope to learn about teacher leadership, supported autonomy, and/or collaboration?

Note

1 Pseudonym, as are all names in this vignette.

References

Campbell, C. (2017). Developing teachers' professional learning: Canadian evidence and experiences in a world of educational improvement. *Canadian Journal of Education*, *40*(2), 1–33. https://doi.org/10.2307/90010103

Croft, A., Coggshall, J. G., Dolan, M., Powers, E., & Killion, J. (2010). *Job-embedded professional development: What it is, who is responsible, and how to get it done well* (Issue Brief). https://learningforward.org/wp-content/uploads/2017/08/job-embedded-professional-development.pdf

Danielson, C. (2007). The many faces of leadership. *Educational Leadership*, *65*(1), 14–19.

Diamond, J. B., & Spillane, J. P. (2016). School leadership and management from a distributed perspective: A 2016 retrospective and prospective. *Management in Education*, *30*(4), 147–154. https://doi.org/10.1177/0892020616665938

Elmore, R. F. (2000). *Building a new structure for school leadership*. www.shankerinstitute.org/resource/building-new-structure-school-leadership

Elmore, R. F. (2005). *School reform from the inside out: Policy, practice, and performance*. Harvard Education Press.

Fullan, M. (2007). *The NEW meaning of educational change* (4th ed.). Teachers College Press.

Krakehl, R., Kelly, A. M., Sheppard, K., & Palermo, M. (2020). Physics teacher isolation, contextual characteristics, and student performance. *Physical Review Physics Education Research*, *16*(2), 1–17. https://doi.org/10.1103/PhysRevPhysEducRes.16.020117

Learning Forward. (n.d.). *Standards for professional learning*. Retrieved May 24, 2024, from https://learningforward.org/standards-for-professional-learning

Learning Forward. (2019). *Meet the promise of content standards: Defining a comprehensive professional learning system*. https://learningforward.org/wp-content/uploads/2017/09/meet-the-promise-of-content-standards.pdfLeithwood, K. A., Mascall, B., Strauss, T., Sacks, R., Memon, N., & Yashkina, A. (2007). Distributing leadership to make schools smarter: Taking the ego out of the system. *Leadership and Policy in Schools*, *6*(1), 37–67. https://doi.org/10.1080/15700760601091267

Marzano, R. J. (2003). *What works in schools: Translating research into action*. Association for Supervision and Curriculum Development.

McKinney, C., Labat, M., & Labat, C. (2015). Traits possessed by principals who transform school culture in National Blue Ribbon Schools. *Academy of Educational Leadership Journal*, *19*(1), 152–166.

Murphy, J., & Hallinger, P. (1988). Characteristics of instructionally effective school districts. *Journal of Educational Research, 81*(3), 175–181. www.jstor.org/stable/40539654

National Association of Elementary School Principals. (1994). *Best ideas from America's Blue Ribbon Schools: What award-winning elementary and middle school principals do.* Corwin Press.

National Association of Elementary School Principals. (1998). *Best ideas for reading from America's Blue Ribbon Schools: What award-winning elementary and middle school principals do.* Corwin Press.

Nerlino, E. (2020). A theoretical grounding of teacher leadership. *Journal of Professional Capital and Community, 5*(2), 117–128. https://doi.org/10.1108/JPCC-12-2019-0034

Perfetto, J., Holland, G., Davis, R., & Fedynich, L. (2013). A comparison of mission statements of National Blue Ribbon Schools and unacceptable Texas high schools. *Journal of College Teaching & Learning, 10*(4), 289–294.

Sahlberg, P. (2021). *Finnish lessons 3.0: What can the world learn from educational change in Finland?* Teachers College Press.

Sahlberg, P., & Walker, T. D. (2021). *In teachers we trust: The Finnish way to world-class schools.* W. W. Norton & Company.

Sinek, S. (2014). *Why good leaders make you feel safe* [Video]. YouTube. www.youtube.com/watch?v=lmyZMtPVodo

T4 Education. (2022). *World's best school prizes.* Retrieved May 24, 2024, from https://t4.education/prizes/worlds-best-school-prizes

Teacher Leadership Exploratory Consortium. (2012). *Teacher leader model standards.* Author. www.nnstoy.org/teacher-leader-model-standards/

Tschannen-Moran, M. (2001). Collaboration and the need for trust. *Journal of Educational Administration, 39*(4), 308–331. https://doi.org/10.1108/EUM0000000005493

Tschannen-Moran, M., & Gareis, C. (2015). Principals, trust, and cultivating vibrant schools. *Societies, 5*(2), 256–276. https://doi.org/10.3390/soc5020256

U.S. Department of Education. (n.d.-a). *Award winners.* Retrieved April 24, 2022, from https://nationalblueribbonschools.ed.gov/awardwinners/

U.S. Department of Education. (n.d.-b). *National Blue Ribbon Schools Program.* Retrieved April 24, 2022, from http://nationalblueribbonschools.ed.gov/home/about-us/

U.S. Department of Education. (n.d.-c). *Practices driving school success*. Retrieved April 24, 2022, from https://nationalblueribbonschools.ed.gov/national-blue-ribbon-schools-a-closer-look/

Visone, J. D. (2018). Developing social and decisional capital in US National Blue Ribbon Schools. *Improving Schools*, *21*(2), 158–172. https://doi.org/10.1177/1365480218755171

Visone, J. D. (2022). Collaborative professionalism in US National Blue Ribbon Schools. *International Journal of Leadership in Education*, 1–22. https://doi.org/10.1080/13603124.2022.2107240

Visone, J. D. (2023). Stepping up and supporting colleagues: Teacher leadership during the COVID-19 pandemic in US National Blue Ribbon Schools. *Leadership and Policy in Schools*, 1–27. https://doi.org/10.1080/15700763.2023.2239898

Visone, J. D. (2024). Teacher leadership for excellence in US National Blue Ribbon Schools. *International Journal of Leadership in Education*, *27*(1), 21–43. https://doi.org/10.1080/13603124.2020.1811897

Wallace Foundation. (2013). *The school principal as leader: Guiding schools to better teaching and learning*. www.wallacefoundation.org/knowledge-center/Documents/The-School-Principal-as-Leader-Guiding-Schools-to-Better-Teaching-and-Learning-2nd-Ed.pdf

Wei, R. C., Darling-Hammond, L., & Adamson, F. (2010). *Professional development in the United States: Trends and challenges*. National Staff Development Council.

Supporting Teacher Leadership for Excellence

"Our teachers need to feel some appreciation, Jim,"[1] asserted an animated Tanya, as she leaned forward in her chair and placed her hands on the edge of Jim's desk. "This pandemic has really affected our teachers, and some are not sure if they will be able to keep doing this!"

Jim was the veteran principal at Elk Grove Middle School. Jim had come to leading Elk Grove after serving as a longtime physical education teacher, coach, and athletic director. He was a fixture within the Elk Grove community, and his popularity was legendary. He responded calmly to Tanya's urgent plea, "What do you suggest?"

"Let those teachers know that they are valued here—that what they are doing is seen and appreciated. Everyone knows the circumstances are not anyone's fault, but they are working so hard, and to know that their efforts are noticed would go a long way."

Tanya's animated and passionate plea continued, though Jim never came around to view this challenge quite as acutely as Tanya did. From Jim's perspective, he was incredibly busy keeping the school operating, dealing with COVID-19 protocols, and managing the work assigned to him by central office. "Touchy-feely stuff" was just not his style.

Jim's responses left Tanya with a choice: she could accept that her school's formal leader was going to trudge along without specifically attending to teachers' mental health and emotional needs, allowing the school's morale to continue to wane, or she herself could do something about it. Tanya, never one to shy away from a challenge, decided to take the latter pathway. Jim, despite his lack of recognition of or motivation to address the issue, did grant Tanya some time at the next faculty meeting to address the challenge as she saw fit.

Tanya enlisted the help of the school's parent teacher organization (PTO). In the coming days, PTO parents visited various businesses in the Elk Grove community. They shared with business owners their wish that the town could show its appreciation for the hardworking teachers who, during the pandemic, put their own and their families' health at risk; served meals to children and families of the school community in the early stages of the pandemic, when schools were closed and students were learning remotely from home; and served as children's personal counselors, as students recounted many challenging situations in their home lives due to the pandemic. The message proved to be persuasive, and the PTO gathered hundreds of dollars in donations for raffle prizes from local businesses (e.g., retail items, gift cards, coupons for services, etc.) that Tanya could include in her teacher appreciation event.

The PTO also contributed many, seemingly random items (i.e., pencils, elastic bands, shoestrings, etc.). Placing these objects in paper bags she gifted to her colleagues, Tanya crafted messages of inspiration for them, using the miscellaneous props as metaphors. For example, she wrote, "It's amazing what you do on a *shoestring* budget." and "*Pencil* in some time for your emotional and physical health."

Tanya explained that she felt compelled to do something because of what she kept seeing on social media. Teachers were leaving the profession. They were quitting left and right. Tanya wondered, "Why are they leaving? Who will take care of these children?" She knew that, with Jim not recognizing the urgency and/or his unwillingness to do something about it, she would need to *step up and do something to support her colleagues* ...

You might be wondering, with some justified righteous indignation: *Why are you highlighting an example where a leader at one of these recognized schools missed an opportunity to support his teachers?* As you uncross your arms, consider that this scenario speaks to the "school next door" characteristic of U.S. National Blue Ribbon Schools (NBRS). They are not perfect. I view this fact as an affirming message for those of us whose schools are less than perfect (Read: ***all*** *of us!*). Despite a missed opportunity by formal leadership, this school was *still able to accomplish great things* because of the first key lesson from the studied NBRS—how *teachers* contributed to the

Table 2.1 The first key lesson about teacher leadership practice in National Blue Ribbon Schools

teacher leadership	Leadership at our school is not limited to individuals with formal titles. Teachers are valued and supported as leaders, and they step up to do what is needed for our collective success.

leadership of their schools, even, in this case, in the face of formal leadership shortcomings. In the scenario above, Jim did not possess the capacity to fulfill all leadership needs in his school. Thus, Tanya, an informal teacher leader, decided to accept the challenge on her own and find ways to show support and appreciation for her teacher colleagues, and the result—NBRS recognition—speaks for itself. Table 2.1 highlights the first key lesson.

Teacher leadership likely exists in all schools in some form or another. However, during my research with NBRS, teacher leadership was highlighted consistently and frequently, illustrating that it was an important ingredient for these schools' success (Visone, 2018, 2023, 2024). Without a proper, supportive culture provided by formal leaders, it is likely that the quantity of teacher leadership, as well as its impact, would be diminished. Even in Tanya's case above, though her principal was not willing to personally assist Tanya, she was permitted to have some time with the staff at the next faculty meeting, and Jim provided her latitude to address the issue in a manner that she saw fit, displaying his trust and empowerment of her. This represents a less-than-ideal means to support teacher leadership, but it is an important, albeit partial, first step. However, based upon my findings, which will be unpacked in the coming sections, this anecdote was an *outlier* in the dataset, with respect to formal leaders' interactions with teacher leaders and their ideas. The overall pattern was much more positive, supportive, and proactive. Let's examine next how the right conditions in NBRS allowed teachers to display leadership.

Supportive Culture for Teacher Leadership

Teacher leadership flourishes and is leveraged effectively when school culture is supportive of teacher leaders' work. Though this statement is likely obvious on its face, some instructive characteristics of these NBRS

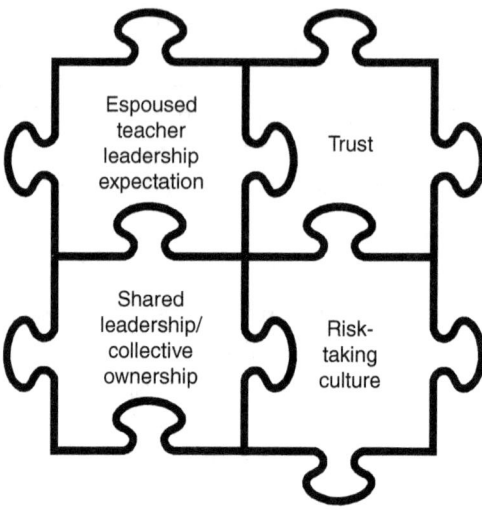

Figure 2.1 Supportive conditions for teacher leadership

manifested a supportive culture for teacher leadership. These conditions toward which your own school can strive, if they are not already present in abundance, are outlined in Figure 2.1 and in the subsequent sections.

Espoused Teacher Leadership Expectations

First, and perhaps, most importantly, these schools had an expectation of teacher leadership. The schools also made the explicit connection that teacher leadership was integral to their success. Teacher leadership was, for these schools, a named "thing." As schools reflected in their applications, every educator was a leader, their staff was a team made up of teacher leaders, and teacher leadership was sought beginning with the hiring process, all indicating that teacher leadership is just a natural way work gets done. Further, a school asserted that teachers were trusted leaders who possessed autonomy related to instructional and management decisions (Visone, 2024). By espousing that teacher leadership is important, a tone can be set about flattening the traditional, hierarchical school structure and about the value of teachers' ideas.

What might this expectation of teacher leadership mean for your school? Perhaps, a quick "non example" anecdote will be helpful. I was speaking with a school principal (not at an NBRS, for clarification), and I asked about teacher leadership at his school. The principal indicated that he was unfamiliar with the concept of teacher leadership. After all, he continued, he leads, and the teachers teach. While this basic statement is not false, given his unfamiliarity with the concept of teacher leadership, it is reasonable to assume that he is not actively using the term with the teachers at his school. Teachers are not hearing from their leader that teachers can be leaders. Teachers are likely not specifically thanked for their leadership when they display it. Teacher leadership is not, for this school, a named "thing." Unfortunately, this is a major missed opportunity. There is so much latent leadership potential in each school among its teachers. However, *teachers are traditionally a humble bunch*. Due to the nature of their overly scheduled days and isolated (from *other adults*, that is!) experiences teaching in their own classrooms, without seeing what their fellow teachers are doing, they frequently come to believe that they do not have anything of value to share with their colleagues or leadership to contribute.

Thus, sometimes, teachers just need to be asked or given permission to lead. For example, for those teachers who believe that they do not have anything of value to share with colleagues, a school leader can affirm instructional practice that is noteworthy and invite the talented teacher to facilitate a teacher-led professional learning experience for colleagues—or simply share what was successful at the next department meeting. "That was great. I would love for you to share this with your colleagues!" sends a message that the teacher has something worthy of sharing and invites teacher leadership. A non-exhaustive list of actions and messages that espouse a teacher leadership expectation are shared in Table 2.2.

In many schools, another group of educators frequently unfamiliar with teacher leadership work (and the named "thing" of teacher leadership) are *teachers themselves*. In addition to being a rather humble bunch, they also do not automatically associate many actions they perform with leadership. For example, teachers might view mentoring colleagues, facilitating professional learning, chairing a committee, organizing a social activity, or providing feedback about the master schedule to administrators, to name a few teacher leadership actions, as just part of their work as teachers. Along similar lines, the same teachers who believe that the list in the last sentence is not leadership work might also view teacher leaders as only those who have a specific title or role (i.e., department chair, teacher leader,

Table 2.2 Actions and messages that espouse a teacher leadership expectation

Conditions Set in Motion by Leaders:
- Leaders "tap" different teachers (as opposed to the *same few*) for various leadership purposes (i.e., committee work, advice, help with something specific, etc.).
- Teachers (not administrators) regularly chair school teams/committees.
- A system of teams/committees includes representation from across the school's teachers.
- The professional learning system includes an expectation that teachers are facilitators of professional learning across different contexts (i.e., communities of practice, workshops, hosting peer observations, etc.).
- The hiring process includes explicitly seeking leadership qualities and experience in new teachers, and teachers participate meaningfully in the process.

Statements by Leaders:
- "Can you help me with something?"
- "I need to borrow your expertise."
- "We need many leaders in many different roles to get the work done."
- "Your ideas are valued and welcome."
- "I would like to recognize <teacher's name>'s leadership on this task."
- "You have something valuable to add. Please share this with your colleagues."
- "We seek leaders at our school. What leadership qualities and experiences can you bring to our team?"

head teacher, etc.) and, accordingly, that these anointed leaders' work is somehow more lofty, important, or valued than the leadership they themselves exhibit informally. At the studied NBRS, teachers and formal leaders were aware of teacher leadership work (that named "thing," again) and could connect their actions to the construct.

In your own school, it would be a valuable exercise to demystify teacher leadership among teachers. This could include reading articles that share examples of teacher leadership in accessible and concise ways. Two favorites of mine are "oldies but goodies" from ASCD's *Educational Leadership* journal. The first, by Charlotte Danielson (2007), entitled "The Many Faces of Leadership," begins by making a solid case for the need for teacher leadership, corroborating the studied NBRS' espousal. Rationales included the impossibly complex and voluminous expectations on principals and other formal leaders, who are sure to need help to get it all done and done well; principals' narrow expertise across the many content areas they are expected to supervise (This former principal and secondary science and social studies teacher is not too proud to admit to this truth!); teaching being a flat profession with few, formal opportunities for growth; and teachers statistically outlasting leaders in their schools many times over. Danielson then proceeded to outline many concrete activities that constitute teacher leadership. These actions included, but were not limited to, assisting leaders with creating the master schedule; serving on a committee to examine a particular schoolwide issue; mentoring colleagues; leading professional learning experiences; creating a parent newsletter at a grade, department, or schoolwide level; and so on.

A second article to generate conversation about what teacher leadership looks like in practice is "Ten Roles for Teacher Leaders" by Cindy Harrison and Joellen Killion (2007), which, like Danielson's article and as its title implies, outlines specific actions that teacher leaders can undertake. Roles that differed from Danielson's list included: resource provider, classroom supporter, instructional/curriculum specialist, data coach, change agent, and learner (which was about modeling proper dispositions and lifelong learning for colleagues). Reading articles such as the two highlighted here, which are concise and practitioner focused, can generate dialogue about creating a culture of teacher leadership.

Standards and tools also exist to help formal and teacher leaders more concretely define leadership work by teachers. One example is the set of *Teacher Leader Model Standards* (Teacher Leadership Exploratory Consortium, 2012), created by a consortium of educational organizations (i.e., public school districts, teacher unions, higher education institutions, educational advocacy and trade organizations, etc.), which outline the work of leading schools and provide examples of how teacher leaders can contribute to this leadership. I have modeled a rubric-like *Teacher Leadership Self-Assessment Tool for Schools* after the Standards, which allows schools (or individual educators) to reflect on their school's (or their own) status and progress with respect to given teacher leadership activities. The full tool can be found in Table 2.3. Also, an editable and printable version of the tool can be found in the Support Material collection for this book.

Table 2.3 Teacher leadership self-assessment tool for schools

Teacher Leadership Self-Assessment Tool for Schools

<u>Purpose</u>: The purpose of the *Teacher Leadership Self-Assessment Tool for Schools* is to allow educators to examine teacher leadership practice in their schools and engender dialogue about ways to maximize the potential of teacher leadership to improve school outcomes. The tool is modeled after the **Teacher Leader Model Standards** (Teacher Leadership Exploratory Consortium, 2012). The citation for these Standards is:

Teacher Leadership Exploratory Consortium. (2012). *Teacher Leader Model Standards*. www.ets.org/content/dam/ets-org/pdfs/patl/patl-teacher-lea der-model-standards.pdf

<u>Directions</u>: Teams of educators or individuals should reflect on each row of the tool, determining which level of practice best describes the current status of teacher leadership in the school (or department, district, or other unit of analysis, including individual teachers examining their own practice). Aim to represent the holistic average of teacher leadership practice. There is no scoring necessary, as this tool is designed to generate conversation about improvement of practice, not label or quantify. In situations where there is more than one idea represented in a "look for" (e.g., from Domain I: "Teachers <u>facilitate some meetings in the school</u> (e.g., <u>committees</u>, <u>teams</u>, <u>PLCs</u>, etc.), <u>generating some buy-in, trust, and/or collective wisdom</u>."), raters can select the column where that particular "look for" is fully realized in practice (e.g., *Limited*), while identifying specific parts of the "look for" in columns to the right, since these elements are more advanced (e.g., *Growing*).

For educator teams, a prompt to consider for each row of the tool could be: *What best represents our school's practice?*

For individual teachers, a prompt to consider for each row of the tool could be: *What best represents my own practice?*

Note that the "look for" descriptions (which are the text in each box in the three right-most columns) are organized along a spectrum of three different proficiency levels of teacher leadership practice: *limited*, *growing*, and *extensive*. Within a Domain, it is likely that "look fors"/rows might be rated at different levels. In other words, not all rows in the same domain need to have the same rating (column). This differential

Supporting Teacher Leadership for Excellence

rating represents the highly contextualized nature of teacher leadership practice. Note also that the use of the word "teacher" in this document is used to mean *any non-administrative-level educator* in a school. This could include classroom, unified arts, and resource teachers; related service personnel; interventionists; school psychologists; social workers; instructional coaches; school nurses; paraeducators; and many others.

How to Use This Tool: Prior to rating within the Standards tool, use the **Supportive Culture for Teacher Leadership Reflective Questions** to examine the cultural context in your school and its potential to support teacher leadership. Next, rate your school's teacher leadership practice via the Standards tool. Once you or your team has reflected upon and rated each "look for," identify a reasonable number of "look fors" (no more than 3–5, to start) that you believe are high leverage and for which you can plan action steps to move your rating farther to the right on the tool. This tool can be reexamined at regular intervals (e.g., annually) to continue your school's progress.

Supportive Culture for Teacher Leadership Reflective Questions:

Directions: Use the **Supportive Culture for Teacher Leadership Reflective Questions** to examine the cultural context in your school and its potential to support teacher leadership. Answer each question by considering your school holistically. For any answers where your honest reflections are less than favorable, determine actionable steps that can move your school toward a more favorable response.

- Is the school culture favorable for *collaboration and teamwork*, as opposed to individualism and competitiveness? Why or why not?
- What is the status of *trusting, professional relationships* among educators at the school (both [a] among teachers and [b] between teachers and administrators)?
- How often is *input* from teachers factored into curricular decisions?
- How often is *input* from teachers factored into non-curricular, schoolwide decisions?
- Could leadership of the school be considered *distributed* or *shared*? Why or why not?
- Does the school culture support teachers' *reasonable risk-taking*?

- Is there an *expectation* that teachers should contribute to the school's leadership? If yes, how is this expectation communicated?
- Are there any *formal structures* to support teacher leadership (i.e., teacher leadership academy, formal and/or informal teacher leadership roles, team/committee systems, school improvement system, etc.)? If so, what are they? If not, why not?
- Are teachers' *talents* and *strengths* known to administrators?
- Are teachers *encouraged* and *invited to participate in leadership* efforts in alignment with their talents and strengths? If so, how? If not, why not?
- Are teachers provided *professional learning* (either formally or informally) to expand their leadership capacity? If so, how? If not, why not?
- Are teachers' efforts to lead *supported* and *appreciated* by administrators? If so, how? If not, why not?
- Are teachers *recognized* for their leadership efforts? If so, how? If not, why not?

Supporting Teacher Leadership for Excellence

Domain	*Limited* Teacher Leadership Practice	*Growing* Teacher Leadership Practice	*Extensive* Teacher Leadership Practice
1. Fostering a Collaborative Culture to Support Educator Development and Student Learning	__ Teachers facilitate few meetings in the school (e.g., committees, teams, PLCs, etc.).	__ Teachers facilitate some meetings in the school (e.g., committees, teams, PLCs, etc.), generating some buy-in, trust, and/or collective wisdom.	__ Teachers facilitate most meetings in the school (e.g., committees, teams, PLCs, etc.), generating buy-in, trust, and collective wisdom.
	__ Teachers rarely assist teaching colleagues and administrators to solve problems, improve the school, and make decisions.	__ Teachers sometimes assist teaching colleagues and administrators to solve problems, improve the school, and make decisions.	__ Teachers frequently assist teaching colleagues and administrators to solve problems, improve the school, and make decisions.
	__ Teachers occasionally model for colleagues effective leadership communication skills (i.e., listening, facilitating, presenting, mediating, advocating, etc.).	__ Teachers usually model for colleagues effective leadership communication skills (i.e., listening, facilitating, presenting, mediating, advocating, etc.).	__ Teachers consistently model for colleagues effective leadership communication skills (i.e., listening, facilitating, presenting, mediating, advocating, etc.).
	__ Teachers infrequently model an appreciation for diverse perspectives and an inclusive culture and rarely use information from diverse perspectives to contribute to fostering understanding and positive interactions among all.	__ Teachers model an appreciation for diverse perspectives and an inclusive culture and use information from diverse perspectives to contribute to fostering understanding and positive interactions among all.	__ Teachers take the lead to appreciate diverse perspectives and an inclusive culture and proactively use information from diverse perspectives to foster understanding and positive interactions among all.
	__ Teacher-led meetings do not exist or are often not productive, unfocused, and/or marked by personal conflict.	__ Teacher-led meetings are inconsistently productive, focused, and conflict (though not disagreement) free.	__ Teacher-led meetings are consistently productive, focused, and conflict (though not disagreement) free.

Copyright material from Jeremy D. Visone (2025), *Teacher Leadership Practice in High-Performing Schools*, Routledge

Teacher Leadership Practice in High-Performing Schools

Domain	Limited Teacher Leadership Practice	Growing Teacher Leadership Practice	Extensive Teacher Leadership Practice
II. Accessing and Using Research to Improve Practice and Student Learning	___ Teachers rarely share research-based strategies or professional learning with colleagues to improve instructional practice.	___ Teachers sometimes share research-based strategies or professional learning with colleagues to improve instructional practice.	___ Teachers frequently share research-based strategies or professional learning with colleagues to improve instructional practice and teach colleagues how to access such resources.
	___ The work of collectively analyzing data to improve student outcomes is either not completed or is not led by teachers.	___ Teachers sometimes lead colleagues in collectively analyzing data to improve student outcomes.	___ Teachers consistently lead colleagues in collectively analyzing data to improve student outcomes.
	___ Teachers do not connect with outside resources (i.e., higher education, community agencies, etc.) for the purpose of improving practice.	___ Teachers occasionally connect with outside resources (i.e., higher education, community agencies, etc.) for the purpose of improving practice.	___ Teachers frequently connect with outside resources (i.e, higher education, community agencies, etc.) for the purpose of improving practice.
	___ Teachers generally do not help colleagues collect, analyze, and use data from their classrooms.	___ Teachers sometimes help colleagues collect, analyze, and use data from their classrooms.	___ Teachers frequently help colleagues collect, analyze, and use data from their classrooms.
III. Promoting Professional Learning for Continuous Improvement	___ Teachers are rarely involved in examining professional learning needs and decisions about future offerings.	___ Teachers are sometimes involved in examining professional learning needs and decisions about future offerings.	___ Teachers are consistently and frequently involved in examining professional learning needs and decisions about future offerings.
	___ Teachers rarely contribute to planning professional learning.	___ Teachers contribute to planning professional learning.	___ Teachers lead the planning for professional learning.
	___ Teachers rarely facilitate professional learning for colleagues.	___ Teachers sometimes facilitate professional learning for colleagues.	___ Teachers regularly facilitate professional learning for colleagues.
	___ Teachers do not advocate for professional learning experiences and structures that reflect best practices (i.e., job embedded, collaborative, sustained over time, aligned with school needs, differentiated, state-of-the-art, etc.).	___ Teachers help advocate for professional learning experiences and structures that reflect best practices (i.e., job embedded, collaborative, sustained over time, aligned with school needs, differentiated, state-of-the-art, etc.).	___ Teachers lead advocacy for professional learning experiences and structures that reflect best practices (i.e., job embedded, collaborative, sustained over time, aligned with school needs, differentiated, state-of-the-art, etc.).

Supporting Teacher Leadership for Excellence

IV. Facilitating Improvements in Instruction and Student Learning	__ Teachers will not offer colleagues constructive feedback on their instruction, or such feedback is not delivered or received positively.	__ Teachers will sometimes offer colleagues constructive feedback on their instruction.	__ Teachers will regularly offer colleagues constructive feedback on their instruction, and such feedback is delivered and received positively.
	__ Teachers do not participate actively in the collection, analysis, and use of data to improve student outcomes schoolwide.	__ Teachers actively collect, analyze, and use data to improve student outcomes schoolwide.	__ Teachers lead the collection, analysis, and use of data to improve student outcomes schoolwide.
	__ Teachers rarely participate in efforts to reflect on peer-observations, examination of student work, analysis of data, and research-based practices.	__ Teachers frequently participate in efforts to reflect on peer-observations, examination of student work, analysis of data, and research-based practices.	__ Teachers lead efforts to reflect on peer-observations, examination of student work, analysis of data, and research-based practices.
	__ Few teachers serve as mentors for less-experienced colleagues.	__ Some teachers serve as mentors for less-experienced colleagues.	__ Many teachers serve as mentors for less-experienced colleagues.
	__ Teachers do not or rarely lead teams, grade levels, and/or departments.	__ Teachers sometimes lead teams, grade levels, and/or departments.	__ Teachers consistently lead teams, grade levels, and/or departments, harnessing colleagues' skills, expertise, and knowledge.
	__ Teachers use technology applications in their instruction, but rarely help colleagues do the same, and do not leverage technology for collaboration and learning beyond the school.	__ Teachers use technology in their instruction, help colleagues do the same, and occasionally leverage technology for collaboration and learning.	__ Teachers consistently and innovatively use technology in their instruction, inspiring colleagues to do the same, and frequently leverage technology for collaboration and learning beyond the school.
	__ Teachers either do not instruct with equity and with meeting individual student needs in mind or might instruct with equity and with meeting individual student needs in mind, but their knowledge is not shared nor modeled for colleagues.	__ Teachers model instruction with equity and with meeting individual student needs in mind.	__ Teachers lead others to instruct with equity and with meeting individual student needs in mind.

Copyright material from Jeremy D. Visone (2025), *Teacher Leadership Practice in High-Performing Schools*, Routledge

Teacher Leadership Practice in High-Performing Schools

Domain	*Limited* Teacher Leadership Practice	*Growing* Teacher Leadership Practice	*Extensive* Teacher Leadership Practice
V. Promoting the Use of Assessments and Data for School and District Improvement	— Teachers may use assessments aligned with state and local standards (both formative and summative), but there is little discussion among colleagues about assessments used. Teachers may rely only on assessments provided from outside sources (i.e., curriculum, administrators, texts, etc.).	— Teachers discuss with colleagues assessments aligned with state and local standards (both formative and summative) for the purpose of selecting and effectively using these measures.	— Teachers initiate and lead discussions with colleagues about assessments aligned with state and local standards (both formative and summative) for the purpose of selecting and effectively using these measures, building colleagues' capacity.
	— Teachers rarely collaborate with colleagues in the design, implementation, scoring, and interpretation of student data to improve educational practice and student learning.	— Teachers sometimes collaborate with colleagues in the design, implementation, scoring, and interpretation of student data to improve educational practice and student learning.	— Teachers consistently initiate and lead collaboration with colleagues in the design, implementation, scoring, and interpretation of student data to improve educational practice and student learning.
	— Teachers contribute to a climate that lacks the trust and critical reflection necessary for challenging conversations about data, which results in limited engagement of colleagues for such challenging conversations about student learning data that lead to solutions to identified issues.	— Teachers create a climate of trust and critical reflection to engage colleagues in challenging conversations about student learning data that lead to solutions to identified issues.	— Teachers create a climate of trust and critical reflection and regularly and respectfully engage colleagues in challenging conversations about student learning data that lead to solutions to identified issues.
	— Teachers rarely work with colleagues to use assessment and data findings to promote changes in instructional practices or organizational structures to improve student learning.	— Teachers sometimes work with colleagues to use assessment and data findings to promote changes in instructional practices or organizational structures to improve student learning.	— Teachers regularly work with and lead colleagues to use assessment and data findings to promote changes in instructional practices or organizational structures to improve student learning.

Supporting Teacher Leadership for Excellence

VI. Improving Outreach and Collaboration with Families and Community	__ Teachers take little initiative to learn about the different backgrounds, ethnicities, cultures, and languages in the school community, resulting in less-than-ideal interactions among colleagues, families, and the larger community.	__ Teachers take initiative to learn about the different backgrounds, ethnicities, cultures, and languages in the school community to promote effective interactions among colleagues, families, and the larger community.	__ Teachers lead colleagues to learn about the different backgrounds, ethnicities, cultures, and languages in the school community to promote effective interactions among colleagues, families, and the larger community.	
	__ Teachers rarely model effective communication and collaboration skills with families and other stakeholders, perpetuating inequitable achievement for certain groups of students.	__ Teachers consistently model effective communication and collaboration skills with families and other stakeholders focused on attaining equitable achievement for students of all backgrounds and circumstances.	__ Teachers assist colleagues to use effective communication and collaboration skills with families and other stakeholders focused on attaining equitable achievement for students of all backgrounds and circumstances.	
	__ Teachers do not or rarely model self-examination of their own understandings of community culture and diversity and how they can develop culturally responsive strategies to enrich the educational experiences of students and achieve high levels of learning for all students.	__ Teachers model self-examination of their own understandings of community culture and diversity and how they can develop culturally responsive strategies to enrich the educational experiences of students and achieve high levels of learning for all students.	__ Teachers facilitate colleagues' self-examination of their own understandings of community culture and diversity and how they can develop culturally responsive strategies to enrich the educational experiences of students and achieve high levels of learning for all students.	
	__ Teachers rarely participate in developing a shared understanding among colleagues of the diverse educational needs of families and the community.	__ Teachers regularly participate in developing a shared understanding among colleagues of the diverse educational needs of families and the community.	__ Teachers take the lead in developing a shared understanding among colleagues of the diverse educational needs of families and the community.	
	__ Teachers rarely collaborate with families, communities, and colleagues to develop comprehensive strategies to address the diverse educational needs of families and community.	__ Teachers sometimes collaborate with families, communities, and colleagues to develop comprehensive strategies to address the diverse educational needs of families and the community.	__ Teachers regularly collaborate with families, communities, and colleagues to develop comprehensive strategies to address the diverse educational needs of families and the community.	

Copyright material from Jeremy D. Visone (2025), *Teacher Leadership Practice in High-Performing Schools*, Routledge

Teacher Leadership Practice in High-Performing Schools

Domain	*Limited* Teacher Leadership Practice	*Growing* Teacher Leadership Practice	*Extensive* Teacher Leadership Practice
VII. Advocating for Student Learning and the Profession	___ Teachers rarely share information with colleagues within and/or beyond the district regarding how local, state, and national trends and policies can impact classroom practices and expectations for student learning.	___ Teachers sometimes share information with colleagues within and/or beyond the district regarding how local, state, and national trends and policies can impact classroom practices and expectations for student learning.	___ Teachers frequently share information with colleagues within and/or beyond the district regarding how local, state, and national trends and policies can impact classroom practices and expectations for student learning.
	___ Teachers rarely collaborate with colleagues to identify and use research to advocate for teaching and learning processes that meet the needs of all students.	___ Teachers sometimes collaborate with colleagues to identify and use research to advocate for teaching and learning processes that meet the needs of all students.	___ Teachers frequently collaborate with colleagues to identify and use research to advocate for teaching and learning processes that meet the needs of all students.
	___ Teachers rarely advocate for students' rights and needs, as well as for resources and support for colleagues, families, and students.	___ Teachers sometimes advocate for students' rights and needs, as well as for resources and support for colleagues, families, and students.	___ Teachers frequently advocate for students' rights and needs, as well as for resources and support for colleagues, families, and students.
	___ Teachers rarely represent and advocate for the profession in contexts outside of the classroom.	___ Teachers sometimes represent and advocate for the profession in contexts outside of the classroom.	___ Teachers frequently take initiative to represent and advocate for the profession in contexts outside of the classroom.

Final Reflection Questions about "Look Fors" beyond the Teacher Leader Model Standards

How frequently do teachers advocate for needs they recognize (i.e., equity, socio-emotional, mental health, teacher appreciation, etc.)?

How frequently do teachers innovate instructional practice among colleagues?

How frequently do teachers take the lead in planning schoolwide programming?

How frequently do teachers serve as a support network for colleagues?

Table 2.3 is a multipage tool that allows individuals or teams of educators to self-assess teacher leadership practice in their schools. The tool first shares a citation and link to the Teacher Leader Model Standards, on which the tool was based, as well as instructions about how to use the tool. The following pages contain a rubric-like tool that spans seven domains of leadership practice and allows educators to rate practice across three different proficiency levels (limited, growing, and extensive teacher leadership practice).

Do not focus too much attention on the ratings assigned when using this tool. Rather, the tool's explicit "look fors" should be used as a framework to generate conversation about how teacher leadership can move forward. First, reflective questions about the culture for teacher leadership found toward the beginning of the tool can provide information about your school's readiness to engage in work to alter or create systems for teacher leadership. For example, if the school culture is highly individualistic and competitive, some attention to team building and non-high-stakes collaboration might be needed prior to attempting to create a data team system. Once the culture is in a more favorable position, teams can more confidently move to more concrete elements in the chart portion of the tool. For example, if your school rated practice in Domain IV (Facilitating Improvements in Instruction and Student Learning) as "Limited Teacher Leader Practice" (e.g., "Teachers rarely participate in efforts to reflect on peer observations, examination of student work, analysis of data, and research-based practices"), your team can select *one* of the best practices cited therein, such as peer observations or examination of student work, and create a system for this practice. A potential trap here that I feel obligated to mention is to rush to create a system for peer observation prior to solidifying the aforementioned culture of collaboration and noncompetitiveness from the prerequisite conditions. Putting the cart before the horse is a likely recipe for failure. Conversely, the tool itself is not sequential, meaning that your school can examine domains (or even rows within domains) in any order. The conversation can begin anywhere your team sees the potential for early wins and meaningful progress. Further, the work on this expansive tool could span several school years. There is much change represented in the tool, and it just might keep your school busy for all of the 5–7 years research suggests are needed for deep change to take root (Wallace Foundation, 2013)!

A final means to manifest your school's expectation of teacher leadership is to celebrate and recognize when teacher leadership occurs. This can vary across different settings, but I will share three varieties that have made a difference for teacher leaders with whom I have worked: small moment recognition, formal recognition within the school community, and formal recognition beyond the school community.

First, small moment recognition involves naming and calling attention to teacher leadership when it occurs in real time. For example, when a teacher offers to create an instructional material to share with her team/department for everyone's consideration at the next meeting, a formal leader should acknowledge the extra effort and connect this action to teacher leadership. "Great leadership, Jen! I appreciate you taking the lead and putting this together for your colleagues," a principal might say. When a teacher is willing to look over a schedule draft and provide feedback, the principal could place a handwritten note in the teacher's mailbox that reads, "Thank you so much for providing me your ideas about the schedule for next year. You raised some crucial points! I appreciate your leadership!" Small moment validation might not have the efficiency of a memorandum to the entire school, but it is the most personal method and can have vicarious effects on those around the teacher leader, such as those teachers who might have been nearby when the principal made such a comment or to whom the praised teacher mentioned the principal's note. We know from foundational social cognitive psychology that vicarious experiences are a powerful motivator and learning tool (Bandura, 1997), so formal leaders' recognition of teachers' micro efforts to lead as important and valued can inspire other teachers to lead, as well.

A related strategy consists of leaders formally recognizing larger leadership efforts by teachers within the school community. Whether this involves a faculty meeting where the principal creates a presentation to acknowledge the hard work of teachers who lead committees and teams, run schoolwide events, and/or facilitate the professional learning of their colleagues, or an email sent to the school following a particular event that highlights specific contributions from teachers, this more formal recognition sends the message to teacher leaders that their efforts are appreciated and seen by administrators. Additionally, the wide distribution of the recognition can, again, have vicarious and inspirational effects on other teachers who were not (yet!) recognized.

Finally, celebration of teacher leaders should occur beyond the school community. This can include such strategies as articles in local newspapers to tout special programs that teacher leaders spearhead and/or presentations to the Board of Education to highlight teacher leaders' work to improve experiences for students in the district. Such sharing beyond the school community is great public relations for your school, and it seems that now, more than ever, public schools and teachers need some positive press and attention!

In a fascinating parallel study from the business world, employees at the large, multinational corporation, Unilever, were asked about their work satisfaction and motivation (Ali & Ahmad, 2009). These dependent (effect) variables were correlated with a series of plausible independent (cause) variables: feelings about work assigned, satisfaction with salaries, opportunity for promotion, recognition for work, working conditions, employee fringe benefits, personal feelings about the job, satisfaction with leadership, and overall satisfaction with the organization. Not surprisingly, all studied variables were positively and significantly correlated with work satisfaction and motivation, meaning that, as one of the variables, say, *satisfaction with salary*, increased, so did the employees' overall work satisfaction and motivation. However, most relevant here is that, of all the variables studied, *recognition* displayed the strongest correlation. *Teacher leaders will be more likely to repeat their leadership if formal leaders merely acknowledge and appreciate their efforts!* It seems too easy to be believed, but this is an opportunity missed by many leaders. Trust me, I know. I hear about this missed opportunity *all the time* from my graduate-level students. These teachers frequently grouse that leaders in their midst do not recognize or appreciate the efforts of teachers. In the studied NBRS, however, recognition of teacher leadership effort was noted consistently. The second condition for supporting teacher leadership in NBRS, a shared leadership/collective ownership ethos, will be discussed next.

Shared Leadership and Collective Ownership

Within the studied NBRS, a team approach was evidenced by a culture of shared leadership and collective ownership over leadership work (Visone, 2023, 2024). One school specifically named both shared accountability and leadership as important. Another discussed their model of shared leadership, which included strategic construction, capacity building for teachers, and opportunities for shared leadership to occur. If someone were to hypothetically ask these schools, "Who is in charge here?", the proper response should be, "We all are!"

This is not to say that there were not formal leaders, titles, and even hierarchies. There were. No need for alarm. I have not discovered schools that have subverted the entire traditional order within them. Principals are still leading schools, but at least at these successful schools, they did not need to (or *want* to) do it alone.

The most commonly identified ways that formal leaders in NBRS shared leadership with teachers and staff was via teams (most frequently including leadership teams) and via "tapping," or inviting leadership participation from teachers. Leadership teams varied in their composition and purpose. Some teams were representational, meaning that they were designed to have a representative from different units of the school (i.e., grade levels, departments, etc.). Others were more focused on a few select members with existing leadership roles (i.e., instructional coaches, reading and language arts consultants, lead teachers, teacher leaders [a formal, identified position, in this case], etc.). Though a more thorough treatment of teaming, including building a system of teams to help lead your school, can be found in my earlier work entitled *Empowering Teacher Leadership: Strategies and Systems to Realize Your School's Potential* (Visone, 2022), it can be instructive to consider how a leadership team operates to maximize its potential to realize shared leadership. For example, Table 2.4 provides a *Leadership Team Analysis Tool* for examining the work of your school's leadership team. Note that, if you are thinking, *we don't actually have a leadership team*, then this tool can help you create one! When using the tool to examine an existing team, think holistically about your typical leadership team meetings. If that is too difficult, consider one particular recent meeting, and analyze that meeting only. Further, once completed for your Leadership Team, this same tool can be easily conceptually adapted to examine the work of any schoolwide team, with the aim of sharing leadership more effectively. An editable, printable version of the tool can be found in the Support Material collection for this book.

A second, less systematic, but no less effective means of sharing leadership is via the tapping of informal leaders to assist with various school operations on an individual basis. A wise leader will get to know the expertise and passions of teachers in the school and tap accordingly. An elementary principal explained to me her use of tapping to empower teacher leadership (after noting that her school can run without her there,

Table 2.4 Leadership team analysis tool

How representative is our team?   Map out team representation by roles (i.e., grade level, department, subject, support roles, noncertified staff, and any other categories you identify).
Who facilitates the discussion within our team?   If there is more than one individual, attempt to outline the percentage of meeting time facilitated by the various individuals.
How does our team spend its time?   Write out general categories of tasks with approximate percentages of time devoted to them (e.g., reviewing minutes, completing paperwork, soliciting input, sharing information, discussion, etc.).
How are our team's decisions made?   (e.g., majority vote, consensus, formal leader decides later, formal leader decides during meeting, etc.)
How participative is our team?   Share the number of times different individuals on the team participated during the meeting, including identifying whether there were members who never shared. Also identify whether you have any norms regarding participation (i.e., everyone answers each question, "monitor your airtime," etc.).
How does our team communicate with the wider school community?   Outline strategies to share the team's work with the rest of the school (i.e., minutes, members share back, formal leaders send a message to all, online posting, etc.).
What ideas or opinions of staff were acted upon by formal leaders?   (i.e., decisions made, new ideas implemented, protocols changed, etc.)   Be honest, and be specific. This is, perhaps, the crux of the tool. Without any action based upon team members' ideas, a leadership team is not sharing leadership, but functioning as a facade of shared leadership.

I might add!). She explained that she doesn't delegate unwanted tasks that she does not want to complete, herself. She empowers her teachers to help in areas where they have strengths and interest. She emphasized that this system was not about taking work off her plate (though that is certain to happen, to a degree), but, rather, this strategy was in service to helping her teachers improve and making the school better (Visone, 2023).

Imagine how empowering this leader's style must be for her teachers! If I am recognized for my interests and/or expertise and provided the opportunity to lead in those areas, it stands to reason that I will be more motivated to perform. Close your eyes, and think of your school. You can most likely picture the faces of teachers who have specific leadership skills (i.e., scheduling, consensus building, written communication, visioning, logistics, parent interactions, etc.). In these highly effective schools, teacher leadership talents like these were leveraged via formal leaders sharing leadership functions with teachers. But, you might ask, *how does sharing leadership affect teachers, given that they are busy enough with their own jobs?*

In an interesting parallel study from the United Kingdom (Quek et al., 2021), an industry experiencing an unfortunate and dangerous turnover rate during the pandemic—nursing—provided a crucial population for determining the effects of shared leadership on rank-and-file employees. The researchers surveyed and interviewed nurses who were involved in an initiative known as the "shared governance framework" (SG), which provided nurses more autonomy and decision-making capability. Nurses involved in SG had more control over outcomes within their health care settings. Nurses were asked to rate various measures of participation and satisfaction with their roles. These nurses' results were compared with those of nurses who were not involved in SG. Not surprisingly, the SG nurses reported higher engagement, empowerment, job satisfaction, and organizational commitment, along with lower turnover intention (the intention to leave their present employer) at statistically significant levels. Similarly, other researchers outside of education have also linked job satisfaction with shared leadership practices (Wood & Fields, 2007).

Within education, Clark-Garcia (2022) found that leaders who support teachers, include them in decision making, and build relationships among educators, help create a *sense of belonging* for teachers. Further, she noted that, when teachers are included in the shared work of the school and feel valued as members of the school community by formal leaders, their *affective commitment* (a measure of how emotionally attached employees are to their workplaces) increases. Considering the teacher recruitment and retention crises presently challenging our profession, I am sure that formal leaders will be most interested in ideas that result in teachers being more satisfied with and emotionally connected to their work. In addition to being standard practice for NBRS achieving exemplary results, this type of culture is a recruitment and retention strategy! To modify a famous line from the 1989 movie *Field of Dreams*: if you empower them, they will stay …

Multidirectional Trust among Educators

The third condition evident in NBRS was multidirectional trust among educators (i.e., teachers trusting teachers, teachers trusting administrators, and administrators trusting teachers). It goes without saying that, for teachers to work collaboratively through peer observations or the examination of student work, as noted in the *Teacher Leadership Self-Assessment Tool for Schools* earlier (Table 2.3), teachers need to trust one another. Additionally, connecting to the shared leadership ethos above, administrators must trust teachers to cede some decision-making control to them. Conversely, to buy into administrators' visions and decisions, teachers should also trust their administrators.

A useful framework for examining trust, which is traditionally applied to teachers' trust in administrators, but can easily be applied across any of the inter-educator trust axes I have outlined above (teacher to teacher, teacher to administrator, administrator to teacher), is called the "Five Facets of Trust" (Tschannen-Moran & Gareis, 2015). The five facets identified by the authors are *benevolence, honesty, openness, competence,* and *reliability*. Benevolence refers to a condition where others can sense that an individual has their best interest at heart. A benevolent administrator or teacher demonstrates care for others. Honesty, though somewhat self-explanatory, includes a strong match between our words and actions. Authenticity and a willingness to "own" mistakes are elements of honesty. Openness involves transparency, as well as displaying trust in others. Competence is about getting the job done and done well. When you can accomplish tasks of importance, others will trust your skill. Finally, reliability refers to follow-through. If others can count on you to do what you say you will, trust will follow.

The discussion of trust above is in service to promoting teacher leadership, as has been exhibited in NBRS. Thus, it can be useful to examine trust through the lens of teacher leadership in your own school. The five facets of trust are applied to teacher leadership in Table 2.5.

Risk-Taking Culture

The final condition in NBRS to support teacher leadership was a risk-taking culture. At the most basic level, teachers in NBRS were permitted to innovate within their instruction, as exemplified by a comment from an elementary school's application to the program noting that teachers can try new strategies and take risks. An elementary principal shared with me why a risk-taking culture required strategic actions by asserting that, without a supportive culture, teachers will not extend themselves in a vulnerable manner to be leaders in front of their colleagues. A secondary principal added that teachers should be able to feel that they can practice leadership without fear of reprisal (Visone, 2023).

Respected educators Ken Kay and Suzie Boss advocated for what they called a "green light culture" (Kay & Boss, 2022), which is a condition where leaders encourage innovation and new ideas. This is consistent with my own advocacy in a prior book for a risk-taking culture to empower teacher leadership (Visone, 2022). Without doing something new, how will we ever get anywhere different from where we are now? How will our persistent achievement gaps ever improve, if schooling proceeds in exactly the same way it has for decades? How will we meet the new challenges of our times, if we apply the same answers we did when teaching with technology meant using an overhead projector or crowding students around a single desktop computer?

Kay and Boss noted that their green light culture involves mistakes and failure. After all, failure can be a powerful learning tool in organizational adaptation and is part of the process of innovating (Heifetz et al., 2009). Thus, formal leaders need to allow teacher leaders to experiment with new ideas. If the trials aren't successful, we put those ideas aside, wiser for our next attempt. To paraphrase that secondary principal above, teachers need to be free to try new things and lead without fear of retribution.

Table 2.5 The Five Facets of Trust, as applied to teacher leadership work

The Five Facets of Trust, as Applied to Teacher Leadership Work*	**Benevolence**
	Does collaborative work result in collective benefits or individual (the requestor's) benefit, only?
	Is possible harm or professional risk likely from others' requests?
	Do educators forgo personal gain in favor of helping the group or others?
	Is proper credit being assigned to those who contribute?
	Are educators looking out for each other's well-being, or is the culture competitive and egocentric?
Honesty	**Openness**
Do educators' words and actions match?	Do explanations represent reality completely?
When educators make mistakes, do they admit to them without blaming others?	When educators identify problems, do they raise and discuss them?
Are educators' communications truthful?	Are educators comfortable sharing opinions with each other, or are conversations guarded?
Is feedback welcomed and both affirming and constructive?	Do some educators stop talking when certain others enter the room?
Competence	**Reliability**
Are educators capable of doing what is asked of them?	Can educators rely on each other to do what each is asked to do?
Do educators work hard?	Are educators' levels of follow-through and effort equitable and commensurate among each other?
Are educators willing to learn what they do not yet know in order to do what is required?	Do educators exhibit consistent follow-through and effort?
Are educators willing to let go of some control when collaborating with others?	

*Based upon the *Five Facets of Trust*, as outlined by Tschannen-Moran and Gareis (2015).

Note. Because teacher leaders' success depends on the work of both teachers and administrators, these questions should be considered with all relationships and combinations of educators in mind (i.e., teacher to teacher, teacher to administrator, administrator to teacher, etc.).

Naturally, administrators cannot say "yes" to every single idea that comes across their desks, lest our schools be in a constant state of amoeba-like flux that will give us motion sickness and render our budgets liquidated by mid-October! After all, some teachers ask for the moon, while others do not have the perspective to consider how their request balances with the other 37-and-a-half requests (roughly) their leader received that same week. However, within reason, formal leaders in NBRS gave their teachers space to create and innovate without fear of reprisal. They often said "yes" to teachers' ideas. (And, not just *saying* yes, but then going ahead and doing something else, anyway!—actually, saying yes, and then following through [recall *reliability* in the Five Facets of Trust] to ensure that the idea was actually implemented!). In your own school, consider how often teachers' ideas are (a) respectfully considered and (b) actually enacted.

Summary

The first lesson learned from NBRS is that leadership in these schools was shared among many individuals, including teachers. Teachers were empowered as leaders. A supportive culture for teacher leadership in these schools included four elements: espoused teacher leadership expectations, shared leadership/collective ownership ethos, multidirectional trusting relationships among educators, and a risk-taking culture.

In creating espoused teacher leadership expectations in your school, it is first important to demystify teacher leadership. Many teachers—a notoriously humble bunch of professionals!—do not recognize actions they perform daily as leadership. Methods to help demystify teacher leadership include: reading literature that shares concrete examples of teacher leadership work; examining standards that outline examples of teacher leadership work; reflecting on teacher practice via the self-reflection tool shared in this chapter (Table 2.3); and naming, affirming, and celebrating teacher leadership when it occurs.

A shared leadership and collective ownership ethos is built over time, including over many small moments that occur each day. However, a structure of representative teams (particularly a leadership team) to help the school accomplish its work can provide teacher leaders forums to express their leadership skills. Another way to formally provide leadership opportunities for teachers is when administrators "tap" teachers to perform leadership roles aligned with their interests and/or expertise. This method requires that formal leaders learn their teachers' strengths and passions and help build teachers' capacities for and interest in leadership.

Multidirectional trust among educators was found across the studied NBRS. The multiple directions included: teachers toward other teachers, teachers toward administrators, and administrators toward teachers. The five facets of trust were shared as a useful lens to examine actions that can lead to trusting relationships. The five facets are: benevolence, honesty, openness, competence, and reliability.

Finally, the supportive climate for teacher leadership in NBRS featured a risk-taking culture. Thus, teachers' ideas for innovating and conducting business differently were often embraced by formal leaders via a green light culture.

Questions to Consider for Chapter 2:

Supporting Teacher Leadership for Excellence

1. Is *teacher leadership* a named "thing" in your school? If it is, how does it present? If not, why not?
2. Is there an espoused expectation of teacher leadership in your school? If so, how is this expectation expressed? If not, what would need to change to espouse this expectation? (Hint: Consider the conditions and messaging in Table 2.2.)
3. Do teachers and administrators understand what teacher leadership is and how teacher leadership practice presents?
4. After reviewing the *Teacher Leadership Self-Assessment Tool for Schools* (Table 2.3), what aspects of teacher leadership practice are:
   a. presently strong and worthy of celebration?
   b. areas for growth?
   c. logical next steps for your school's focus?

5. Following up Question 4, what are concrete steps (i.e., systems to create, committees to form, practices to implement, goals to set, data to gather, etc.) you and/or your school can take to move forward within a particular row on the *Teacher Leadership Self-Assessment Tool for Schools* (Table 2.3)?
6. What systems and/or teams exist in your school to allow for shared leadership and/or collective ownership? If few exist, what systems for this purpose could you develop?
7. Considering the Five Facets of Trust, how would you assess the level of trusting professional relationships in your school? (Consider teacher to teacher, teacher to administrator, and administrator to teacher.)
8. Are teachers comfortable taking reasonable professional risks in your school? If so, what contributes to their comfort? If not, what is holding them back?

Note

1 Pseudonym, as are all names and places in this vignette.

References

Ali, R., & Ahmad, M. S. (2009). The impact of reward and recognition programs on employee's motivation and satisfaction. *International Review of Business Research Papers*, 5(4), 270–279.

Bandura, A. (1997). *Self-efficacy: The exercise of control*. W.H. Freeman & Company.

Clark-Garcia, A. (2022). *The effects of distributed leadership on organizational commitment for public school teachers*. Central Connecticut State University.

Danielson, C. (2007). The many faces of leadership. *Educational Leadership*, 65(1), 14–19.

Harrison, C., & Killion, J. (2007). Ten roles for teacher leaders. *Educational Leadership*, 65(1), 74–77.

Heifetz, R., Grashow, A., & Linsky, M. (2009). *The practice of adaptive leadership: Tools and tactics for changing your organization and the world*. Harvard Business Press.

Kay, K., & Boss, S. (2022). *Redefining student success: Building a new vision to transform leading, teaching, and learning*. Corwin.

Quek, S. J., Thomson, L., Houghton, R., Bramley, L., Davis, S., & Cooper, J. (2021). Distributed leadership as a predictor of employee engagement, job satisfaction and turnover intention in UK nursing staff. *Journal of Nursing Management, 29*(6), 1544–1553. https://doi.org/10.1111/JONM.13321

Teacher Leadership Exploratory Consortium. (2012). *Teacher leader model standards*. Author. www.nnstoy.org/teacher-leader-model-standards/

Tschannen-Moran, M., & Gareis, C. (2015). Principals, trust, and cultivating vibrant schools. *Societies, 5*(2), 256–276. https://doi.org/10.3390/soc5020256

Visone, J. D. (2018). Developing social and decisional capital in US National Blue Ribbon Schools. *Improving Schools, 21*(2), 158–172. https://doi.org/10.1177/1365480218755171

Visone, J. D. (2022). *Empowering teacher leadership: Strategies and systems to realize your school's potential*. Routledge. https://doi.org/10.4324/9781003190370

Visone, J. D. (2023). Stepping up and supporting colleagues: Teacher leadership during the COVID-19 pandemic in US National Blue Ribbon Schools. *Leadership and Policy in Schools*, 1–27. https://doi.org/10.1080/15700763.2023.2239898

Visone, J. D. (2024). Teacher leadership for excellence in US National Blue Ribbon Schools. *International Journal of Leadership in Education, 27*(1), 21–43. https://doi.org/10.1080/13603124.2020.1811897

Wallace Foundation. (2013). *The school principal as leader: Guiding schools to better teaching and learning*. www.wallacefoundation.org/knowledge-center/Documents/The-School-Principal-as-Leader-Guiding-Schools-to-Better-Teaching-and-Learning-2nd-Ed.pdf

Wood, M. S., & Fields, D. (2007). Exploring the impact of shared leadership on management team member job outcomes. *Baltic Journal of Management, 2*(3), 251–272. https://doi.org/10.1108/17465260710817474

Stepping Up to Get Stuff Done

"We're struggling to figure out what this should look like, Tina,"[1] Jasmin stated honestly during her Grade 2 data team meeting at Northwest Elementary School in early September. The team was having difficulty transitioning their traditional math instructional model to a workshop approach, which was now a district expectation. Tina, their principal, was attempting to support the team, though she knew just slightly more about the model than her teachers. Her support had consisted of providing materials, articles about math workshop, professional learning workshops, and lesson ideas. This school year was designed to be one of learning and trial and error. However, the second-grade team was experiencing setbacks, struggles, and an inability to put the many elements of a functional math workshop (e.g., guided math small group instruction, math workstations, student independence, etc.) into practice. The team was stuck—with one notable exception. Kiersten had conducted some research on her own and had been tinkering around with her math workshop. She was starting to see some solid results. Namely, student independence had increased, and fewer students were struggling with taught concepts. Not wanting to elevate herself above her respected colleagues, she sheepishly answered Jasmin, at a volume barely above a whisper, "I think I have a pretty good system working in my room, and the kids seem to be getting a lot out of it." Heads all swiveled toward Kiersten.

"Really?!" questioned Jasmin, feeling just a bit embarrassed that she had so boldly generalized her team as struggling, while her colleague was finding success.

"Can we see what you are doing?" asked Todd, figuring that he wanted to replicate what Kiersten was doing, and the best way to accomplish this was by seeing Kiersten's class in action.

"Yeah, I would love to see that," chimed in the final teammate, Rebecca.

"Sure," Kiersten replied with a bit more confidence, given the enthusiasm from her teammates.

"Do you think we can go and see Kiersten's room and what she is doing?" asked Jasmin, turning back to Tina.

"Definitely. I want to learn, too." Tina indicated that she would make it happen. The following Tuesday, Northwest's Grade 2 team and Tina watched Kiersten operate her math workshop. The team took furious notes. The visitors crouched beside students' desks, asking students questions and observing work at their level. Students were more than happy to share their learning with other teachers and their principal.

Tina had also arranged for coverage for Kiersten, so that, immediately following the team's visit, the entire group could meet in the office conference room to debrief what they had observed and ask Kiersten questions. During the debriefing session, after a prolonged period of effusive praise and gratitude to Kiersten for her work to set up the math workshop so successfully and willingness to host her teammates and principal, the group peppered Kiersten with logistical questions made possible because the group now knew more about the model, having *seen* it in operation. The learning was deep and meaningful to the team, who wanted to know how and where to start making this happen in their own classrooms. When Tina finally asked what next steps each teacher might consider, based upon what they had seen in Kiersten's room, the group articulated myriad concrete responses. They were ready to make changes—*that day*.

Over the next few weeks, as Tina visited the Grade 2 classrooms for informal and formal observations during math time, she noticed something she had not in the past few months—*consistency*! The team, upon witnessing Kiersten's model in real time, brought similar structures and styles back to their own classrooms. Tina was so proud of the effectiveness of this embedded professional learning. It was so fortunate, she figured, that Kiersten had expertise to share with her colleagues—*expertise that Tina did not possess* …

How Teacher Leadership Manifests

In this chapter's vignette, we met a grateful principal, Tina, who was delighted that one of her teachers possessed an instructional expertise that she did not. What a relief for Tina! Kiersten could *show* her colleagues how to run a math workshop, as opposed to Tina's ability to *tell* them about one, based upon her reading about the structure. As with the vignette in Chapter 2, we witness a teacher leader stepping up to fill a need in her school. Again, the principal, though well meaning, does not have all that her teachers need. Thus, teacher leadership is critical to maximize the group's, and, ultimately, the children's, success.

The U.S. National Blue Ribbon Schools (NBRS) I studied exhibited robust teacher leadership work across several key categories: instructional leadership, decision-making, innovation, and beyond the walls of the school (Visone, 2023, 2024). These categories are consistent with comprehensive reviews of the field of teacher leadership (Nguyen et al., 2020; Wenner & Campbell, 2017; York-Barr & Duke, 2004); standards for teacher leadership (Teacher Leadership Exploratory Consortium, 2012); practitioner-based articles that help demystify teacher leadership by providing concrete examples (Danielson, 2007; Harrison & Killion, 2007); and recent, research-based frameworks about teacher leadership work (Bae et al., 2016; Berg & Zoellick, 2019). Recall the first key lesson from my research with NBRS was about the support for and presence of teacher leadership. See Table 3.1 for this key lesson.

Chapter 2 dealt with the supportive culture for teacher leadership in NBRS. In this chapter, I will share four major categories of teacher leadership found in NBRS and discuss implications for your school. The four categories are: *instructional leadership*, *decision-making*, *innovation*, and

Table 3.1 The first key lesson (again) about teacher leadership practice in National Blue Ribbon Schools

teacher leadership	Leadership at our school is not limited to individuals with formal titles. Teachers are valued and supported as leaders, and they step up to do what is needed for our collective success.

instructional leadership	decision-making
innovation	leadership beyond the school

Figure 3.1 Four main categories of teacher leadership found in National Blue Ribbon Schools

leadership beyond the school. Figure 3.1 shares the four main categories of teacher leadership found in NBRS.

Teachers as ... Instructional Leaders

As in the vignette for this chapter, one of the most prominent means for teachers to display leadership was by serving as instructional leaders for their colleagues. This should not come as a big surprise since teacher leaders are, first and foremost, *teachers*, meaning that their expertise is primarily and necessarily rooted in their work in classrooms to influence student learning. Figure 3.2 outlines the various ways teachers manifested instructional leadership in NBRS. This is, by no means, an exhaustive list, nor is it meant to limit the conversation on how instructional leadership should look in your school. Rather, these are the ways instructional leadership manifested in these schools.

The most frequently identified instructional leadership category was activity under the sprawling umbrella of professional learning. For this discussion to resonate, we need to be clear about what professional learning includes. Research about effective professional learning tells us that it should be deeply connected to teachers' daily work (*You mean that it is not learning something today that you might use only once four months from now?!*); be collaborative (*You mean teachers don't learn best by keeping what they learn to themselves?!*); be intertwined with teachers' work, over time (*You mean explaining something new to teachers one time the day before school starts won't result in successful implementation throughout the year?!*); and should leverage principles of adult learning (*You mean that administrators and/or consultants don't know everything, and teachers can bring valuable knowledge and skills to professional learning situations?!*), among other characteristics (Croft et al., 2010; Garet et al., 2001; Learning Forward, n.d.).

Stepping Up to Get Stuff Done

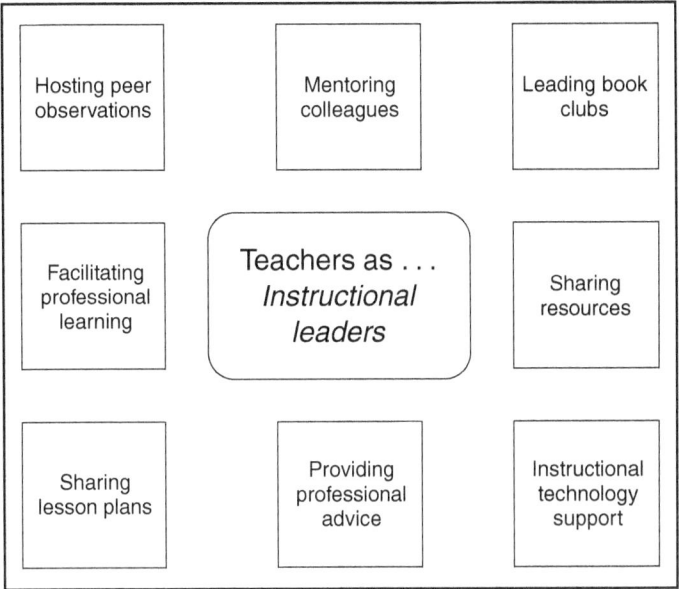

Figure 3.2 Ways teachers manifested instructional leadership in National Blue Ribbon Schools

There were many ways that teachers in NBRS facilitated the learning of their peers. In the most authentic example, as consistent with the vignette for this chapter, teachers learned by *watching each other teach* through peer observations. One school noted in its application that teachers would observe each other, provide coaching feedback from the visits, and make changes accordingly to their instruction (Visone, 2024).

In other works, a colleague and I share a specific model of peer observation that was used for professional learning when I was principal of an NBRS (Mather & Visone, 2024a, 2024b; Visone, 2016, 2020, 2022a, 2022b). We called these learning opportunities *collegial visits*. The visits were focused upon a need determined by the group of teachers or our instructional leadership team. Most often, the volunteer teacher who agreed to host the visit was trying something new that we had recently learned about, so *she was not expected to be an expert* when opening her classroom to colleagues. The visit itself would last about 30 minutes, so we could see a complete, or nearly complete, lesson. Following the classroom visit, we held an immediate debriefing session that included *all* present, especially the host teacher, where we discussed what we saw.

55

Notice that I am using the pronoun "we," meaning that I too, as the principal, participated in the visits and debriefing sessions. ... Once you have administered smelling salts or poured an icy bucket of cold water over your head to return you to consciousness following this shocking revelation, take some slow, deep breaths and allow me to explain. I did not participate so I could hold my teachers accountable or evaluate their performance. I participated so I could *learn* from and alongside them. However, we had to build the multidirectional trust referenced in Chapter 2 before we could successfully include me on the visiting team.

Collegial visits are deeply connected to teachers' daily work, are a collaborative experience, yield opportunities to follow up prior learning (and provide touchstone experiences for future conversations), and are reliant on the expertise of teachers. Check, *check*, **check**, and <u>check</u>, when we compare collegial visits to the characteristics of effective professional learning. Most relevant to my research in NBRS was that many of these schools leveraged a system of peer observation for the purpose of professional learning.

Another way teachers exhibited instructional leadership was via facilitating professional learning in more traditional ways, such as leading workshops, book clubs, and smaller instructional team meetings. An elementary principal shared his opinion that having teachers facilitate professional learning displays leaders' trust in teachers (See Chapter 2 for a discussion of multidirectional trust supporting teacher leadership), but, more importantly, teachers facilitating colleagues' learning increases buy-in because teachers are more apt to listen to a fellow frontline educator (Visone, 2023). This is not to say that presenters and experts from outside your school cannot add meaningfully to the group's learning. (This would be a very self-defeating position for me to take, given my present role as a faculty member in higher education!) However, a professional learning system that *regularly includes teacher voice and leadership* is a solid investment in building teacher leadership capacity and provides your teachers with relevant, relatable, and impactful professional growth. Further, consider the wide breadth of expertise you have among teachers in your school, which can provide for many more varied professional learning options for teachers, and which can, in turn, allow for more teacher choice in their learning. This is another hallmark of an impactful (and popular!) professional learning system.

Table 3.2 can be used to audit professional learning forums and expertise among your staff for facilitation. The tool can assist your school in increasing professional learning leadership from educators other than administrators, widening the pool of expertise, increasing the volume of offerings to encourage choice, empowering teacher leaders, and providing your hard-working administrators some relief from the pressure that they need to be the source of (or pay for!) all professional learning. Note that an editable and printable version of this tool can be found in the Support Material collection for this book.

Teachers in NBRS also learned from one another in other, less structured ways. For example, they shared lesson plans and resources, and they provided their colleagues with professional advice on a wide range of topics, including classroom management, engagement with parents, and instructional strategies. Further, teacher leaders both formally and informally mentored colleagues. Since some of my research took place at the height of the COVID-19 pandemic, one particular area of support that was noted repeatedly was assistance in the use of technology for instruction. The pandemic created a unique situation, where some of the most experienced teachers were novices with respect to the technology toward which the entire profession had abruptly pivoted. As a result, some of the newest (read: *younger*) teachers possessed an expertise their veteran colleagues did not and were running workshops. In some schools, the traditional, symbolic relationship between age and expertise was turned completely on its head! Thus, the pandemic provided a space for new teacher leaders to emerge, as the usual suspects for teacher leadership were less equipped to lead. The unprecedented nature of the remote teaching environment broke down some of the preexisting teacher leadership expectations and hierarchies. Teacher leaders had to step up to help each other, and teachers with less experience than ever were doing so, thanks in part to the pandemic. Further, as with the vignettes from Chapters 2 and 3, teacher leaders at NBRS stepped up to fill needs that no one else (including their principals) could (Visone, 2023).

Teachers as ... Decision-Makers

Teachers also displayed leadership as decision-makers within their schools. Building and central office administrators still had the final say,

Table 3.2 Professional learning audit tool for teacher leadership

List all professional learning opportunities in our school over the past school year. Next to each opportunity, identify when teachers or other nonadministrative staff members* facilitated the experience, alone or as part of a team. (e.g., workshops, book clubs, learning communities, peer observations, etc.)
Consider individual teachers' and other nonadministrative staff members' areas of expertise. What are strengths and possible areas for instructional leadership? Name specific individuals, along with their expertise. (e.g., Nghi Lam [Gr. 4]: differentiation of assessments; Carlos Gonzalez [social worker]: restorative practices)
Outline how professional learning opportunities that are offered are decided. Who makes these decisions? (e.g., committee, administrators, survey, exit slips from professional learning experiences, etc.) **How can this process become more participative?**
What professional learning forums presently exist for teachers and other nonadministrative staff members to share their expertise? (e.g., required workshops, faculty meetings, grade-level or department meetings, learning communities, optional workshops, summer learning opportunities, book clubs, etc.)
Based upon the information above, create a plan to increase teacher and other nonadministrative staff member facilitation of professional learning. (e.g., system for peer observation, book clubs, rotational guest speaker at standing meetings, sign-up for optional workshop facilitation, teacher choice workshop day, etc.)

*Nonadministrative staff members might include certified staff who do not have administrative responsibilities, such as psychologists, instructional coaches, resource teachers, counselors, social workers, related service personnel, nurses, etc. They could also include noncertified staff, such as paraeducators, tutors, administrative assistants, etc.

and teachers were not "in charge." However, consistently and across many different examples, teachers provided input into decisions, and, often, made important decisions, themselves.

One unique manifestation of teachers' decision-making was illustrated during the COVID-19 pandemic. Namely, after relatively ubiquitous school closures and remote learning, school districts across the United States needed to plan carefully for their reopening at various points during the pandemic, the timing depending on the appetite of the community, public health experts' views, politics, and many other complicated factors. Teachers, who were by no means experts in matters of public health (though they were *no less* expert than their administrators and, frankly, *all of us* who lack degrees in epidemiology!), were increasingly becoming experts at the unfolding reality of remote teaching, in addition to their previous expertise about what teaching looked like before the pandemic. Thus, NBRS, like so many schools and districts across the United States during this time, created reopening committees that included heavy teacher representation (Visone, 2023).

These committees debated and advised about the particulars of running schools during a pandemic, from the spacing of desks and chairs in classrooms, to the logistics of operating lunch waves, to ways to warmly and enthusiastically welcome children back to their schools. Yes, the U.S. Centers for Disease Control and Prevention set the general parameters, but it was up to local committees to implement these larger recommendations on a granular level. The once-in-a-lifetime (hopefully!) nature of this situation meant that teachers were helping lead through an adaptive challenge, defined by Heifetz et al. (2009) as a challenge that is only adequately addressed through changes in people's beliefs, through what they see as important, and through loyalties.

As in the case of facilitating professional learning outlined above, to affect teachers' beliefs and priorities to realize adaptive change, it is important to obtain teacher buy-in. A secondary school explained how their staff views the positive relationship between decision-making input and teacher buy-in. The school asserted that teacher ownership of and participation in decision-making leads to their greater investment. A secondary teacher leader noted a more practical reason for formal leaders wanting teachers' input, when she shared that her administrators welcome her and her colleagues' opinions, since the administrators are no longer in the classroom (Visone, 2023). Teachers, particularly since the pandemic, have expertise and frontline knowledge that their administrators do not possess.

An elementary principal shared how such decision-making assistance looks in practice. Namely, he assembles a teacher leadership team to participate in two-way dialogue and decision-making about any new initiatives. In most cases, NBRS included a system of standing teams/committees, often headlined by a leadership team. These teams provided forums for the solicitation of teacher input, systems of communication to the rest of the staff, and opportunities for teachers to have leadership roles within them (i.e., chairing a team, leading a subcommittee or project, etc.). As noted in Chapter 2, this type of system was a concrete manifestation of a shared leadership culture.

Figure 3.3 provides a set of questions that can help you explore the role of teachers as decision-makers in your school. First, you will need to consider what forums exist for teacher input into decision-making, as well as how often teachers' ideas are acted upon. The set of questions ends with a number of specific prompts regarding how teachers provide input based upon a set of leadership areas of responsibility, as outlined by standards for educational leaders (National Policy Board for Educational Administration, 2015).

What forums exist for teacher input into decision-making, in general, across the school?

Within these forums, how often are teachers' ideas acted upon?

What input can teachers have into . . .

    the school's mission, vision, and goals?

    curricular, instructional, and/or assessment matters?

    equity matters?

    student support matters?

    the professional community of teachers matters?

    operations and management matters?

    parent and community engagement matters?

    school policy matters?

Figure 3.3 Guiding questions about teachers as decision-makers

Teachers as ... Innovators

We will never see results different from the ones we have already seen unless we do things differently from how we have always done them. In Chapter 2, one cultural element present in NBRS was a risk-taking culture that provided teachers in these schools the space and confidence to experiment with new ideas without fear. The tangible result of this culture of experimenting with new ideas was that teacher leaders served as innovators in their schools (Visone, 2024). An elementary principal shared that her teachers continually have new ideas they want to try, and they bring these ideas to her collaborative forums for implementation (Visone, 2023). Specific examples of teacher-led innovations in NBRS have included a school partnership with local manufacturing companies, where students collaborate with businesses on design challenges; a kitchen-themed mathematics course; improvements to the mathematics student intervention system; and a plethora of instructional technology applications, many of which were necessitated by the adaptive change of remote teaching during the pandemic.

Maybe you are the creative, innovative type. Perhaps, you are not. No judgment here. Regardless of your own ability to envision doing things differently, within your school, there are undoubtedly creative, innovative educators, some of whom might not be expressing their talents to their fullest. It is important to provide support, forums, and recognition for their innovation, lest they feel stagnated or, worse yet, *leave*. The tool in Table 3.3 can help you examine possibilities for innovation. Note that an editable and printable version of the tool can be found in the Support Material collection for this book.

The tool in Table 3.3 is organized to move you from your present reality to a more innovative potential. First, use the top section to identify innovations that were initiated by teachers. Then determine whether their innovation has been recognized and, if not, determine a means to do so. Next, look to present systems and forums to determine where innovation can be encouraged and discussed. This will help identify existing conditions to support innovation, or it will provide you the space to create such a system. Finally, the bottom section can be used to identify, based upon knowledge of your school's staff or, perhaps, based upon input from your school's staff, what potential exists for innovation among teachers. Once

Table 3.3 Teacher leader innovation efforts inventory

Teacher Leader Innovation Efforts Inventory		
Innovation	Teacher Leader Innovator	Recognition Provided or Potential for Recognition

Teacher Leader Innovation Forums
To what teams/committees/forums or to whom can teacher leaders bring ideas for innovation? What does the approval process look like?

Teacher Leader Innovation Ideas
Describe the idea, identify the teacher leader, and share what might need to occur (i.e., permissions, pilot testing, buy-in from others, information sharing, etc.) prior to the innovation's initiation.

Innovation 1:

Innovation 2:

Innovation 3:

concrete ideas are identified, along with the individual teacher leaders who could champion these ideas, you can outline a "road map" of what must occur (including actions you would need to undertake) to support and nurture these innovations. Table 3.3 can help formal leaders and leadership teams support teacher leadership innovation in their school, which is "win-win," as the school will improve what it does, while building leadership capacity in others and buy-in for the new ideas (since the innovations do not belong to administrators). The next section will outline the final significant category of teacher leadership activity in the studied NBRS: leadership beyond their schools.

Teachers as ... Leaders beyond Their Schools

In the studied NBRS, teachers' leadership did not stop at the schoolhouse door. Teachers in these schools displayed leadership in many forums and organizations beyond their schools. These leadership manifestations were wide ranging, both in content and scope, but in most schools, these beyond-school leadership opportunities started within their districts and communities.

From an instructional leadership perspective, teachers in NBRS were looked upon to share ideas and practices with colleagues across their districts. Naturally, any instructional leadership by teachers overlaps with the category of the same name discussed earlier, but I highlight the following example here, as this theme is about teacher leadership beyond teachers' own schools, and, in this case, teacher leaders spread their influence to wider audiences. Specifically, one elementary school's application explained that teachers provided professional learning to not only their own school, but also to colleagues across the district.

Another source of community leadership was via family and community engagement. Examples here were, again, widespread, but they included organizing and facilitating family and community events on behalf of their schools, sharing ideas with next year's teachers about effective ways to work with particularly challenging family situations, communicating with families regarding the importance of school attendance, and providing ideas for the use of technology for family communication during the pandemic. There were also deeper engagements with communities that went beyond school. For example, one principal explained how the teachers at his secondary school stepped up to fill a need in the community by serving meals to families during the COVID-19 pandemic. He noted that teachers were not asked to do this, but rather they chose to on their own, displaying leadership and a willingness to do whatever it took to help their students and families. A secondary teacher leader, whom you read about in the vignette for Chapter 2, used her position as a teacher leader to rally the community to show its gratitude for the school's teachers by collecting donations from local businesses for use in a teacher appreciation raffle. She told her school's professional development committee, before heading out to the community to seek donations, that she was insisting that they do something to address teachers' emotional and mental health. She emphasized that they needed to be appreciated and validated (Visone, 2023).

Teacher leaders also led beyond their communities. Within the studied NBRS, I found teacher leadership in the form of serving on statewide curriculum committees, allowing other schools to come observe their collaborative practices, serving in leadership roles at state and national levels, participating in the creation and scoring of standardized assessments, writing for publication, and winning prestigious awards (Visone, 2024). These are but a few of the specific ways that teachers displayed leadership beyond their schools. It can be insulating working at a school, especially if a teacher has no other experience outside that school or district. Teachers, like all of us, do not know what we do not know. So experiences with those outside our comfortable working environment can guard against professional myopia. Encouraging teachers to advance their knowledge and careers by participating in professional learning outside their district, attending graduate classes, connecting with professional organizations, to name a few ideas, can help broaden teachers' perspectives and provide them with prospects for expressing their leadership to new audiences and for different purposes. In my aforementioned book about empowering teacher leadership (Visone, 2022a), I devote the entire final chapter to teacher leadership beyond the school, providing tips and templates for presenting to boards of education, presenting at conferences, writing for publication, and testifying about educationally relevant bills in the state legislature, among other ideas.

How Do Teachers Lead in Our School?

Up to this point in the chapter, you have learned how teacher leadership manifested in NBRS. This knowledge is not especially useful by itself. The practices at these schools are only useful if you can move your school's culture toward one where this type of leadership occurs with regularity. In Chapter 2, Table 2.3 was presented as a means to spark conversation about teacher leadership practice, based upon the Teacher Leader Model Standards (Teacher Leadership Exploratory Consortium, 2012). Table 2.3 is a tool you can use to show what teacher leadership can be and to provide a rubric-like road map to track your school's (or individual teacher leaders') journey over time. However, your school might also take a more inductive or grassroots approach to building a teacher leadership culture like that found in NBRS.

Table 3.4 provides a series of survey items a school could use to solicit input from teachers about potentially interesting teacher leadership activities. Note that I would treat this survey as an *optional* ask of teachers. Teacher leadership is not for everyone, and, particularly for new teachers, they might be more in need of help and mentorship than they are ready to provide it! In a macro sense, this information could help a school's leadership team plan systems, forums, committees, opportunities, and so on to match what teachers are sharing as their interests and areas of expertise. Further, leaders will know what professional learning topics (i.e., professional learning facilitation, budgeting, parent engagement, public speaking, data-driven decision-making, etc.) will be necessary to help teachers attain their stated teacher leadership intentions. Consider Table 3.4 a needs assessment for capacity building. In the micro sense, leaders can now know whom to "tap" when they are confronted with challenges that require a team approach. Note that an editable and printable version of the survey items can be found in the Support Material collection for this book.

Table 3.4 Teacher leader talents and interests inventory

Directions: This **optional** brief survey is to assist our leadership team in creating a culture of teacher leadership. We are stronger and more effective when many are leaders. Research has shown that teacher leadership is an important part of the culture of highly successful schools, and our leadership team seeks to understand the unique talents and interests of our staff. Please answer the following items to help us learn about how you wish to contribute. Naturally, since this is a means to get to know our talents and interests on an individual level, we are asking you to first tell us who you are. This will allow us to follow up with you.
Please share your name: _____
Please select *all that apply* for the following items.

	I am interested in contributing to our school through:
	Instructional Leadership: o leading professional learning o hosting peer visits to my classroom o writing curriculum o mentoring a colleague o leading a book club o sharing resources and/or lesson plans with colleagues o providing instructional technology support o offering instructional advice to colleagues
	Decision-Making Leadership: o joining a committee/team (Name committee/team here: _____) o planning an event (Name event here: _____) o providing my input on _____ (Name topic here: _____)
	Innovation Leadership: o We can improve _____. (Name topic here: _____) o I have an idea I would like to discuss with you. o We need to change something. (Name thing here: _____) o I tried something new, and it worked great! I would like to share.

> **Leadership beyond the School:**
> o I lead _____ outside our school. (Name leadership here: _____ _____)
> o I would be willing to share _____ to others outside our school. (Name topic here: _____)
> o Our school should share _____. (Name topic here: _____ _)
> o I am interested in presenting, but I would need some assistance.
> o I am interested in writing, but I would need some assistance.
> o The community needs _____, and I can help.
>   (Name need here: _____)
>
> **What do you feel you need from our leadership team to contribute in the ways you listed above? Please help us understand how we can help you.**
> (examples could include: professional learning, opportunities, coaching assistance, resources, time, etc.)

Summary

The first key lesson from research on NBRS was about teacher leadership. It asserts in full: leadership at our school is not limited to individuals with formal titles. Teachers are valued and supported as leaders, and they step up to do what is needed for our collective success. Chapter 3 outlined teacher leadership manifested by NBRS in four main categories: *instructional leadership, decision-making, innovation*, and *leadership beyond their school*.

Teacher leadership via instructional leadership, intuitively, was the most observed category of the four. This leadership often took the form of facilitating professional learning, mentoring other teachers, sharing lesson plans and resources, hosting colleagues to view their teaching, leading book clubs, offering pedagogical advice, and providing instructional technology assistance. Professional learning leadership was particularly prominent in the dataset. Research has noted that the most effective professional learning is collaborative, ongoing, deeply connected to the daily work of teachers, and reflective of adult learning principles, among other qualities. Teacher leaders are uniquely positioned to provide professional learning that meets these best practices, since they know best about their daily professional learning needs, are present with colleagues when embedded professional learning needs arise, and can work collaboratively to push their teams' collective learning forward. One particular professional learning structure highlighted in NBRS that leverages all the aforementioned best practice qualities is peer observation, where teachers can learn by observing each other's instruction. A tool (Table 3.2) allows schools to examine their professional learning structures to determine how to maximize teacher participation in the facilitation of peer's learning.

Teachers also led through participation in school decision-making. Given that some of the research occurred during the height of the COVID-19 pandemic, many NBRS highlighted the role of teachers in reopening committees in their schools and districts. The most common way teachers expressed decision-making leadership was through participation on committees and teams. A tool (Figure 3.3) allows schools to examine how teachers are invited to provide decision-making input in a variety of important leadership areas.

Teachers in NBRS were innovators for their schools. Innovations involved instructional matters, primarily, but also included developing partnerships with outside organizations. A tool (Table 3.3) allows schools to inventory prior teacher-led innovations, reconsider their system for harnessing teacher-led innovations, and create plans to support particular teacher-led innovations.

Teachers in NBRS were also leaders outside their schools. This began in most NBRS in their own communities, where this leadership meant everything from sharing resources and ideas with teachers across the district, to organizing events for families, to handing out meals to families as volunteers during the pandemic. Other teacher leaders were involved with educational organizations at their state or national level and/or were recognized for their excellence with awards. Still others shared their work and learning in the form of presentations or publications.

Chapter 3 concluded by connecting teacher leadership manifested in NBRS to teacher leadership work occurring (or soon to occur!) in your school. A tool (Table 3.4) provided an optional survey to collect data about what teacher leadership skills exist, what leadership interests your school's teachers possess, and how you can help nurture the leadership of teachers in your building.

Questions to Consider for Chapter 3:
Stepping Up to Get Stuff Done

1. Describe the professional learning "system" at your school and/or district.
    a. How are topics selected?
    b. Who plans professional learning experiences?
    c. Whose perspectives are considered? Whose are not considered?
    d. Who facilitates professional learning experiences?
    e. How are connections made among professional learning experiences, school/district aims, and teachers' daily work?
    f. In what forms does professional learning manifest? (i.e., workshops, staff meetings, professional learning communities, book clubs, peer observations, lesson study, coaching, etc.)
    g. What is missing from your professional learning system to help it be the best it can be?
2. How can you maximize teacher participation in facilitating professional learning?
3. Identify how teachers are instructional leaders in your school. Be as specific as you can. What is your vision about what teachers' instructional leadership can become?

4. Considering your responses in Figure 3.3 about teacher input into decision-making, what are two areas where you believe teacher input should be included more than it is now? How can this increased input be accomplished?
5. Innovations help schools move forward and do differently to achieve better results for students. Considering your responses to Table 3.3 prompts, what can you do to encourage and support teacher innovation? What teacher-led innovations do you believe will significantly move your school forward?
6. By positioning themselves as leaders outside of their own schools, teacher leaders can bring back new ideas to their schools, furthering innovation. Which of the teachers in your school are presently in a position to learn new ideas beyond your school (i.e., graduate courses, participation in educational organizations, presentations/publications, social media, etc.)? How can the school leverage and/or learn from their experiences?
7. How can formal leaders in your school partner with teachers for leadership experiences beyond your school (e.g., presenting at conferences, writing for publication, applying for grants, etc.)?

Note

1 Pseudonym, as are all names and places in this vignette.

References

Bae, C. L., Hayes, K. N., O'Connor, D. M., Seitz, J. C., & Distefano, R. (2016). The diverse faces of teacher leadership. *Journal of School Leadership, 26*(6), 905–937. https://doi.org/10.1177/105268461602600602

Berg, J. H., & Zoellick, B. (2019). Teacher leadership: Toward a new conceptual framework. *Journal of Professional Capital and Community, 4*(1), 2–14. https://doi.org/10.1108/JPCC-06-2018-0017

Croft, A., Coggshall, J. G., Dolan, M., Powers, E., & Killion, J. (2010). *Job-embedded professional development: What it is, who is responsible, and how to get it done well* [Issue Brief]. https://learningforward.org/wp-content/uploads/2017/08/job-embedded-professional-development.pdf

Danielson, C. (2007). The many faces of leadership. *Educational Leadership*, 65(1), 14–19.

Garet, M. S., Porter, A. C., Desimone, L., Birman, B. F., & Yoon, K. S. (2001). What makes professional development effective? Results from a national sample of teachers. *American Educational Research Journal*, 38(4), 915–945. www.jstor.org/stable/3202507

Harrison, C., & Killion, J. (2007). Ten roles for teacher leaders. *Educational Leadership*, 65(1), 74–77.

Heifetz, R., Grashow, A., & Linsky, M. (2009). *The practice of adaptive leadership: Tools and tactics for changing your organization and the world*. Harvard Business Press.

Learning Forward. (n.d.). *Standards for professional learning*. Retrieved May 24, 2024, from https://learningforward.org/standards-for-professional-learning

Mather, B. R., & Visone, J. D. (2024a). Peer observation to foster collective teacher efficacy: Teachers' perceptions about collegial visits. *Journal of Professional Capital and Community*, 9(2), 85–104. https://doi.org/10.1108/JPCC-08-2023-0057

Mather, B. R., & Visone, J. D. (2024b). Peer observation to foster teacher self-efficacy. *Journal of Educational Research & Practice*, 14(1), 1–22. https://doi.org/10.5590/JERAP.2024.14.1.01

National Policy Board for Educational Administration. (2015). *Professional standards for educational leaders*. https://doi.org/10.24627/sswc.10.0_125

Nguyen, D., Harris, A., & Ng, D. (2020). A review of the empirical research on teacher leadership (2003–2017): Evidence, patterns and implications. *Journal of Educational Administration*, 58(1), 60–80. https://doi.org/10.1108/JEA-02-2018-0023

Teacher Leadership Exploratory Consortium. (2012). *Teacher leader model standards*. Author. https://www.nnstoy.org/teacher-leader-model-standards/

Visone, J. D. (2016). A learning community of colleagues enhancing practice. *Kappa Delta Pi Record, 52*(2), 66–70. https://doi.org/10.1080/00228958.2016.1156511

Visone, J. D. (2020). Pre-launch preparations for a peer observation initiative viewed through a concerns model. *Professional Development in Education, 46*(1), 130–144. https://doi.org/10.1080/19415257.2019.1585385

Visone, J. D. (2022a). *Empowering teacher leadership: Strategies and systems to realize your school's potential.* Routledge. https://doi.org/10.4324/9781003190370

Visone, J. D. (2022b). What teachers never have time to do: Peer observation as professional learning. *Professional Development in Education, 48*(2), 203–217. https://doi.org/10.1080/19415257.2019.1694054

Visone, J. D. (2023). Stepping up and supporting colleagues: Teacher leadership during the COVID-19 pandemic in US National Blue Ribbon Schools. *Leadership and Policy in Schools*, 1–27. https://doi.org/10.1080/15700763.2023.2239898

Visone, J. D. (2024). Teacher leadership for excellence in US National Blue Ribbon Schools. *International Journal of Leadership in Education, 27*(1), 21–43. https://doi.org/10.1080/13603124.2020.1811897

Wenner, J. A., & Campbell, T. (2017). The theoretical and empirical basis of teacher leadership: A review of the literature. *Review of Educational Research, 87*(1), 134–171. https://doi.org/10.3102/0034654316653478

York-Barr, J., & Duke, K. (2004). What do we know about teacher leadership? Findings from two decades of scholarship. *Review of Educational Research, 74*(3), 255–316.

Supported Autonomy
An Empowering Balance for Teachers' Practice

"Take out your formative assessment data, everyone," requested Dani,[1] who was the math department chair at Rolling Valley High School. Teachers in the geometry data team scrolled, clicked, and searched on their laptops until the requested spreadsheets were located. "What do you see in the dataset?"

"My students certainly have zero understanding of the types of transformations and their features," observed Amber.

"Same here," agreed Solomon, nodding affirmatively.

"I see the same thing," noted Nylah, "but I must point out that we haven't taught that material, yet. I mean, it makes sense that our kids don't know what they are doing with translations, as we are still working on the foundational content of angles. The students have struggled with that, a bit, so we gave them more time with that content."

"This is good to know, Nylah, but the curriculum pacing guide indicates that we should have begun this unit a few weeks ago," Dani chided. "I found a way to get my class to start the new unit, after a brief review of the angles content they needed." Dani taught one class section of geometry, while the others had two to three classes, each.

"How did you do that?" wondered Solomon. "Why don't we spend our time today figuring out how you got your students to move forward from angles, so we can get our kids to a similar place?" Nylah and Amber agreed with Solomon that it would be worthwhile to shift the focus of the meeting to address a problem they recognized in all their classes (except for Dani's, of course). Amber pointed out that this time spent backtracking might be well spent, as it would help students with the content they will soon experience.

"Well, I can send you some resources, perhaps," replied Dani, "but we need to take a look at our content standards in the new unit today." Dani was concerned that looking back at content she had already pushed to the rearview mirror would leave the team behind in their sequencing. She also wondered about the productivity of their meetings. If they veered too far from the stated agenda this time, it might set a precedent to veer more often. Dani craved order and routine, and, given her students' success with angles, she thought that Solomon's suggestion would not be the best use of time.

With noticeably less enthusiastic participation, the geometry data team soldiered forward. Amber and Solomon sent each other messages via their laptops to share their displeasure with Dani's decision. Formative assessment results related to the new unit were begrudgingly examined, and plans to teach these concepts were developed, mostly by Dani. The math team adjourned at the sound of the bell without much discussion, with its members heading out to teach as they were instructed.

Across town, the Riverbend Middle School English Language Arts Grade 8 team gathered in their planning room. There are no department chair positions at the middle school level, so one of the school's building leaders, an assistant principal, Jeff, was charged with supporting the group. However, on this day, Jeff was dealing with a significant investigation of potential bullying on one of the school's buses, and he was presently interviewing students and watching video of the bus ride, as the team's time began with the bell. Jeff was present for Grade 8 ELA meetings approximately one-third of the time; thus, his leadership was not predictable nor particularly helpful, as he was not knowledgeable about most of the group's work.

"What are we supposed to do today?" conscientious veteran Tricia inquired after the group exchanged pleasantries and expressions of exhaustion near the conclusion of a challenging week teaching eighth graders.

"I think we are supposed to discuss our benchmark data," answered Jannelle.

"Well, I don't have mine ready, yet," remarked Tim. "I was running behind in the curriculum, and I did not think it was fair to the kids. Besides, I did not know we were going to talk about it today, anyway. There was no agenda, was there?"

"No, but Jeff did mention it last week," noted Brenda.

"Well, that would explain it, as I was out last week. I had that curriculum meeting at central office, remember?" Tim stated. "It doesn't make a lot of sense to go over those results today, since we don't all have them ready." The group used about 10 minutes of their meeting to debate the merits of examining benchmark data that were available (all teachers' classes but Tim's). Most were in favor of doing so, given that general patterns could be determined. However, in the end, Tim convinced the group to wait, especially since Jeff was not there, anyway.

The group shifted focus to discuss an upcoming unit, where a few teachers shared how they address specific concepts with their classes. However, no consensus was reached on any particular strategy. The sharing was more in passing and "for your information" than it was for decision-making purposes.

With about seven minutes left in the team's meeting time, Jeff stopped by the planning room, seemingly out of breath. "Sorry I am late. I had an issue to deal with. What have you been working on?"

Jannelle offered Jeff a three-minute rundown of the team's discussion topics, including that they pushed examination of benchmark data to the following week, given that not all data were available yet, and Jeff had not been there to discuss them, anyway.

Jeff, whose head was spinning with witness statements, silent bus video footage, and anticipated forthcoming uncomfortable conversations with parents, was half listening to Jannelle's summary. He felt much too guilty about only arriving with a few minutes remaining in the meeting to offer anything but superficial and supportive comments regarding the decision to postpone the discussion of benchmark data. His limited understanding of the team's ineffective, passive, and nonconsequential idea sharing for the upcoming unit positioned him such that he could not offer any meaningful feedback about that conversation either. Thus, he mostly nodded as Jannelle spoke and counted the minutes down until he could get back to his investigation. After a few more minutes of general and noncommittal discussion about the upcoming unit, the bell rang, and the team adjourned for the week without having accomplished anything of value.

This vignette was a tale of two teams. I will note that these two teams were *not* found in U.S. National Blue Ribbon Schools (NBRS). However, they can help us understand a key lesson I learned from NBRS.

It is human nature to compare and rate. Therefore, which team is of more interest to you, either from a teacher or an administrator perspective? Rather than impose my own opinion here, I will help unpack the characteristics of each, based upon what we learned of their work during one meeting.

At the high school geometry data team meeting, we witnessed a group that was organized and ready to present their formative assessment data, as planned. Leadership was present and willing to facilitate the meeting. We learned about a leader who was willing to support the group with resources. We also observed teacher leadership dispositions, whereby teachers were honest about their students' lack of success, about being behind in the curriculum pacing, and about their willingness to learn from a colleague about how to achieve better results.

On the other hand, we also witnessed a leader who was more concerned with order and routine than a legitimate, shared need for the vast majority of students represented by the team. We also learned about a leader unwilling to let the group's collective ideas steer the group, in favor of her own ideas. Finally, and likely resulting from Dani's rigidity with respect to the team's work, we found a group moving passively through begrudging compliance.

This is not a team of which most of us want to be a member, on either side of the desk. The teachers did not feel empowered, as their voice and ideas were stifled. Dani, though she might have felt satisfied that she "got her way" in this particular meeting (undoubtedly a short-term win, only), will likely soon find this group to be less participative and not terribly invested in what is becoming "Dani's work" (undoubtedly a long-term loss).

Shifting our focus to the middle school ELA team, that group also displayed some teacher leadership, in that they needed to carry the meeting forward while their assigned leader, Jeff, was often unable to attend. There was also teacher autonomy to make decisions, given Jeff's absence. Finally, there was an open sharing within the meeting, where the group was focused on "the work," which, in this case surrounded teaching an upcoming unit.

However, the middle school team had plenty of challenges as well. Again, their assigned leader could not commit to consistent, full-time presence, and there was a general lack of order, expectations, and accountability for the group. Thus, their time, precious as common planning time is, devolved into a low-stakes and nonconsequential conversation *about the work*, as opposed to *doing the work*. Jeff, as a leader, has not built any credibility or dependability with the Grade 8 ELA team to offer any meaningful suggestions, and it is likely this team will not accomplish much more together than they can as individual teachers.

In short, you have likely decided that neither of the two teams is ideal, and I wholeheartedly agree with you. The high school math data team is very leader-centric, with Dani providing much order and structure, and even support. However, she is doing so without allowing for much voice from the rest of the group. The other teachers were merely passive members, rather than true participants and team members. They complied, for now, and they might accomplish some meaningful work for their students, but the teachers (aside from Dani) will not be invested in the work. The middle school ELA team was devoid of leadership, order, structure, and accountability. Though they had great autonomy, by default, this autonomy was not accompanied by much support or expectation. This team will likely not accomplish much together, but on the bright side, they will not be overly stressed about it.

What is missing in these situations is related to the second key lesson from my research with NBRS. This lesson is about setting in motion a system of teacher work that is (a) supported by structures, systems, and leadership (both formal and informal) and (b) marked by a high degree of teacher autonomy, within the parameters set in motion by (a). This second lesson is illustrated in Table 4.1.

Table 4.1 outlines the concept of *supported autonomy*, which I am defining as the ideal balance of leadership support and trust in teachers. Within supported autonomy, teachers are provided the material resources, time, answers to questions, effective systems, and other supports (such as from their colleagues) needed to teach and collaborate. Beyond this support, leaders trust teachers with the "how" of instruction and collaboration. Teachers are treated as professionals. Before we examine what

Table 4.1 The second key lesson about teacher leadership practice in National Blue Ribbon Schools

supported autonomy	Teachers at our school are provided the supports they need to effectively educate students. However, teachers are trusted by leaders to determine how to best meet students' needs.

supported autonomy looked like in NBRS, I want to begin by exploring autonomy as a construct, both beyond and within education.

Who's the Boss of Us?

In the legal realm, autonomy can be considered as one acting on one's own free will, as opposed to others' will (Parchomovsky & Stein, 2021). These authors note the word's etymology from the Greek words for "self" and "rules." In more common parlance, an autonomous individual might say, "I'm the boss of me!" As human beings, our autonomy is usually limited as children (thankfully!), when our whims and curiosities might lead us to more adventure (as well as mischief and danger!) than we are ready for (at best) or to an untimely demise (at worst). Either way, adults in our lives help guide us to the point where we can eventually meet our own needs, make responsible decisions (hopefully!), and become autonomous individuals (Snedden, 2013). For teachers working in a school, the autonomy in question is *professional autonomy*.

The medical field, as an example outside our profession, presents an intriguing study of professional autonomy. Doctors enjoy an unusual degree of independence from management compared with most other professionals, with their supervision coming mainly from "self-control and social mechanisms" (Salvatore et al., 2018, p. 1). In these authors' study, doctors identified more with their organizations (i.e., hospitals, clinics, etc.) if they experienced autonomy in their daily work and decision-making. Though the comparison to the highly professionalized nature of the medical field is not a completely analogous one for education, the general finding that, as autonomy rises, so do positive feelings of connectedness toward one's organization, is important and more than relevant to educators. Again, recall my findings in Chapter 3 that teacher leaders in NBRS served as innovators and decision-makers, which are manifestations of professional autonomy in education. However, before we delve into teachers' autonomy in schools, what is professional autonomy?

Elston (1991), writing about the medical field in the United Kingdom, provides this helpful definition of professional autonomy: "Professional autonomy refers to the legitimated control that an occupation exercises over the organization and terms of its work" (p. 61). The degree of professional autonomy within a field is thought to be influenced by a variety of factors, not the least of which are economic (such as supply and demand—the *rarer* someone's talent/expertise, the more autonomy they might possess in their work) and societal (How much does a society *value* the work of a profession? Does the society *trust* the expertise of a particular profession?).

Professional autonomy is not such a natural fit within PK–12 education because of the traditional, top-down culture. Further, in the current societal climate, public education is having a moment of declining respect in the United States (Natanson, 2022), so it is hard to envision societal pressure having a positive influence on teachers' autonomy any time soon. Yet in other societies, teachers occupy a different (Read: *better*) status than they do in the United States (Sahlberg & Walker, 2021). For example, in Finland (See Chapter 1 for another brief discussion of schooling in Finland and why we can learn from what they do.), teachers possess an elevated societal standing compared to what they experience in the United States. In fact, the first part of the title of Sahlberg and Walker's (2021) work, *In Teachers We Trust*, tells us what we need to know, relative to this discussion, about how Finland views its educators. To compare the United States across more nations, this highlight from the Organisation for Economic Cooperation and Development's *Education at a Glance 2021: OECD Indicators* report for the United States (2021) speaks volumes ("Highlight" is the authors' term. I argue that it should be affectionately reclassified as a "*low*light"!):

> Teachers in the United States have some of the lowest actual salaries compared to those of tertiary-educated workers on average in the OECD. In 2019, US teachers' salaries ranged from 59% to 66% of the earnings of tertiary-educated workers on average at pre-primary, primary and general secondary levels of education, whilst the OECD average range was from 81% to 96%. (p. 1)

Ouch. This finding means that, when comparing the United States to countries with a wide range of profiles (from Germany, Japan, and the United Kingdom to Colombia, Mexico, and Türkiye), teacher salaries are lower in the United States in relation to other professions that require a college degree. Certainly, this is a manifestation of the importance U.S. society places on the teaching profession. Thus, if professional autonomy is to be granted to teachers, it will likely need to come from *within* the profession, not externally, such as from society, at large.

The late, great educational thinker Richard Elmore made a connection between teacher autonomy and societal expectations (Elmore, 2005). He described a phenomenon known as "loose coupling." He paradoxically noted the low societal standing of the teaching profession: "teaching was thought [by society] not to require expertise on a level with other, 'real' professions" (p. 45), while also sharing that teachers, in practice, are actually insulated by administrative interference to protect teachers' autonomy in their classrooms from outside scrutiny. He continued to explain that loose coupling explains why many educational reform initiatives fail—there is too much room for teachers to opt out of doing what is asked of them (Read: *autonomy*).

To be fair, Elmore's critique is about two decades old, at the time of this book's publication, and much has changed to tighten the loosely coupled system against which he opined. Principals' roles in this system have shifted from mere managers and keepers of order to instructional leaders, whose influence on student outcomes is second only to the teachers themselves (Leithwood et al., 2004; Marzano et al., 2005; Wallace Foundation, 2013). Even more recently, a comprehensive and authoritative updated report by the Wallace Foundation concluded that the influence of principals as found in their own earlier studies were likely *underestimated* (Grissom et al., 2021)! Thus, gone are the days when principals merely left teachers alone and protected them from outside influence (at least, at the most effective schools). Further, teacher evaluation changes have attempted to define more concretely what good teaching looks like and what supervisors like principals should be expecting when they visit classrooms (Hill & Grossman, 2013). The intersection of an increasingly professional teacher workforce, convergence of expectations on what good teaching is, and teachers' ability to make decisions based upon their professional knowledge, but within the parameters of professional expectations, is where supported autonomy lies. Michael Fullan (2007) observed that "the solution to motivating people is to establish the right blend of tightness and looseness" (p. 43). That balance is represented by supported autonomy. This chapter will later outline how administrators and teaching colleagues can set up conditions and expectations where teachers have the support they need to teach with effectiveness and to act as professionals, with flexibility for teachers to chart the specific pathway for their work and student learning.

Autonomy for Teachers, as Considered by Others

Others in education have specifically considered the construct of professional autonomy, with respect to teachers. Before we learn how this presented for teachers in NBRS, it will be instructive to see how others have viewed this concept before.

First, we might consider what teachers themselves think about autonomy with respect to their practice. In a very interesting study from Wales, Hughes and Lewis (2020) chronicled a large-scale curriculum overhaul. Teachers were provided ready-made curriculum units, which, on the surface, might seem to be a source of tension with respect to teachers' professional autonomy, as this level of prescription could narrow the scope of teachers' pedagogical decision-making. However, the authors found that teachers actually *appreciated* the ready-made curricula, as these materials were seen as an efficient solution, as opposed to starting with no curriculum and having to create everything themselves. Thus, teachers in this study were willing to trade some aspects of their professional autonomy when the right support was provided. The authors recommended that teachers be provided curricular support, both in the form of ready-made materials and units, which would save teachers time, and via ongoing professional learning and opportunities to debrief, which is consistent with what is known about the collaborative and iterative nature of effective professional learning (Learning Forward, n.d.). I don't want to jump ahead too much, as I plan to share what I learned about NBRS practices, but this study from Wales (Hughes & Lewis, 2020) seems to point us directly to the *supported autonomy* I will outline shortly. Specifically, the authors advocated for upfront and ongoing support, while teachers were provided with autonomy to determine how to use the resources and their learning.

More broadly, another study shared teachers' attitudes about autonomy (Strong & Yoshida, 2014). They measured teachers' levels of autonomy with respect to curriculum (similar to Hughes & Lewis, 2020), professional development, classroom management, student assessment, and schoolwide operations. Strong and Yoshida (2014) found that teachers reported the highest levels of autonomy within the area of classroom management, and elementary teachers reported less autonomy than secondary teachers in general. They recommended principals and other educational leaders provide teacher leadership opportunities to share leadership work and decision-making, which might, in turn, improve teachers' commitment to collaboration and the school's mission. When we examine NBRS findings below, you will likely think that NBRS were paying attention to Strong and Yoshida's (2014) recommendations!

Hargreaves and O'Connor (2018) outlined a form of teacher professional autonomy in a work about their broader concept of *collaborative professionalism*, a construct we will unpack more directly in Chapter 5. In their model, they describe *collective autonomy*, which is one of 10 tenets of collaborative professionalism. According to the authors, collective autonomy occurs when "educators have more independence from top-down bureaucratic authority, but less independence from each other. Teachers are given or take authority" (p. 6). In such situations, there is accountability from the collective, what we might call collective ownership, whereby the success of all students is dependent on the work of all teachers, not just teachers working with individual students. In our chapter vignette, teachers should be completing their assessments with students in collaboration with colleagues' schedules, not so much because their formal leaders told them to, but because they do not wish to let their teammates down, and there is important work that follows review of and is contingent on completing these assessments that will directly impact student learning. In simpler terms, *we work for each other, ultimately for the kids*. This lens focuses most on teachers and their interactions with one another, where the supported autonomy we will consider below also reflects the teachers' interactions with their formal leaders, as well.

Another respected leader in our field, Michael Fullan, shared a different style of autonomy. He outlined *connected autonomy*, whereby groups of educators leverage their collective learning to improve their autonomous work (Fullan, 2019). In short, the better a group collaborates, the more they learn and the more individually effective they can be. They will leave collaboration opportunities with more information to positively influence their decision-making. We will learn more about this type of collective learning in Chapter 5, when we explore collaborative professionalism in NBRS.

Speaking of collaboration and its relationship to autonomy, Vangrieken et al. (2017) aimed to reconcile a seeming paradox when collaboration and autonomy are juxtaposed. Traditional views of autonomy evoke images of independence and individualism, which seem antithetical to collaboration, where educators work together via interdependence. However, the authors note that the concept of autonomy in psychology has several different aspects, including *reactive autonomy*, which connotes the individualistic, non-reliant actions of the aforementioned traditional view, and *reflective autonomy*, which includes interdependence and choice over actions that can occur in groups just as well as it can occur for individuals (Koestner & Losier, 1996). Thus, Vangrieken et al. (2017) concluded that the concepts of autonomy and collaboration can be reconciled by applying principles from the subcategory of reflective autonomy. In other words, teachers can experience autonomy in their collective work, just as they can have it as individuals. Collaboration will also be a primary focus of Chapter 5. Next, we will examine what I found in NBRS with respect to teachers' supported autonomy.

Strategic Structures for Excellence

The first word in *supported autonomy* is "supported." Thus, we will first examine how NBRS created supportive conditions that led to teachers experiencing autonomy. First, we will discuss logistical conditions I found (Visone, 2018, 2022a).

Formal leaders in NBRS set in motion a variety of supportive structures that allowed for autonomous teacher work. First, there were forums in which Fullan's (2019) aforementioned connected autonomy could occur. Examples of such forums included professional learning communitie; staff meetings; professional learning workshops; and grade-level and/or department meetings, under the wider umbrella of common planning time, where teachers could work together on common goals. Closely related were early-release days set aside for teacher professional learning and collaboration. Nothing shared here is especially unique or beyond the norm, which I argue is a most encouraging point. There is nothing that these schools were doing with regard to structures and schedules that cannot be replicated in any school setting. Though these steps are not grandiose, the lowest level of support toward teacher autonomy in NBRS were forums for collaboration. Vangrieken et al. (2017) would likely be impressed by the strategic and peaceful coexistence of collaboration and autonomy in NBRS. Without these forums for collaboration, connected autonomy would have to occur on teachers' own time. We know that teachers learning from each other happens organically, in practice, but to see it occur at scale and strategically, we need leaders' support to put it on the calendar. We will examine the work within these forums a bit later.

Beyond the forums listed above, NBRS also displayed evidence of systems thinking (more on this in Chapter 5), where other forums for collaboration could support teachers' autonomy. Examples of these systems were creating a schedule of meetings during which teachers could discuss intervention needs and progress of their students, empowering teachers to serve as representatives for their grade levels or departments on various teams and committees, and building a system of interconnected teams to allow for shared and distributed leadership to occur across many facets of the school's work. Note that a more complete discussion of creating a system of teams to support teacher leadership and participation in school decision-making can be found in my most recent book: *Empowering Teacher Leadership: Strategies and Systems to Realize Your School's Potential* (Visone, 2022b). Once again, all these structures are fairly standard practice in most schools, which is good news for those looking to build a structural foundation for supported autonomy. An elementary principal explained that, with different educators' interests and areas of strength, there is a means, such as through committees, for all teachers to contribute to the school's leadership, encapsulating the way the studied NBRS attempted to use structures and systems to maximize teachers' leadership potential. Naturally, the principal continued, these committees and other forums for teacher leadership built collegiality and relationships across the school (Visone, 2022a). Speaking of collegiality and relationships, we will next examine the relational aspects of supported autonomy, which is where NBRS might separate themselves from some other schools (but, not from *yours*, of course!).

Back to Trust Again

In Chapter 2, I introduced elements of multidirectional trust for empowering teacher leadership. When considering supported autonomy in NBRS, trust, again, proved a key construct (Visone, 2018, 2022a). Essentially, without administrators trusting their teachers (recall Finland's educational atmosphere referenced earlier), there would be no autonomy. Teacher leaders noted a lack of micromanagement from their administrators, reflecting administrators' trust in them. They used language that connoted their ability to steer their classrooms in the right direction, possession of academic freedom, and ability to explore within the bounds of their curricula (Visone, 2022a).

Further, an elementary school's application spoke to the manifestation of administrative trust in teachers, whereby the leadership team empowers teachers to make decisions and implement them (Visone, 2018). A secondary school even included the term *autonomy* in their description of teachers' ability to procure resources. An elementary school's application also spoke specifically to autonomy with respect to a professional learning library of videos showing colleagues' instruction. The school explained this library provided teachers autonomy to chart the course of their own professional learning. A secondary school principal considered autonomy from the lens of professionalism, stating that, by treating teachers as professionals, he was giving them the freedom to operate their classrooms as they believed was best for their students (Visone, 2022a).

Specifically with respect to teacher collaboration, two elementary principals explained how teachers' autonomy also belonged in teacher meetings. The first noted that administrators were present during teachers' collaborative meetings, but teachers ran them. The second consciously stepped back from running the meetings to provide teachers with choice and a safe collaborative environment that is flexible and teacher driven (Visone, 2022a).

These findings from teacher leaders and administrators in NBRS exemplify supported autonomy. Teachers are provided structures, forums, and trust in their decision-making (as well as *capacity* to do the work, through professional learning)—this is the *support*. Then they are allowed to make decisions without strict oversight, which is the *autonomy*. Next, we will consider how this balanced condition can manifest in a noticeable element of teachers' work—*collaboration*.

How Supported and/or Autonomous Are Our Teachers?

In this chapter's opening vignette, two different teams were presented. Neither of the groups had an ideal combination of support and autonomy. The high school math group was primed to follow data to guide their work for the betterment of their students, but they were held back because their leader was unwilling to veer from her own agenda. They exhibited support (I would suggest that the "support" for this team was more like "control.") from their leader. However, they did not have autonomy. The second group was the middle school English Language Arts team. They had tremendous autonomy and freedom to drive their work. However, their group lacked leadership direction and support. Though their assigned administrator supported their autonomy by not getting in the way, he was unable to contribute meaningfully to their work, mostly due to his general absence from discussions, and, as such, their "support" was more in the form of a negative—lack of oversight. In contrast to these two less successful teams, what if we applied the lessons of supported autonomy to teachers' forums for common planning time?

Figure 4.1 displays a quadrant diagram for considering the work of teachers in their common planning time meetings. To make sense of the diagram, a few terms should be contextually defined. First, *content* in this context refers to both the topics discussed and the overall flow of the meeting, including who is leading the meeting, how decisions are being made, how collaborative the work is, and so on. Second, *coherence* here refers to the status of the collaboration content, across and within meetings. In other words, is the flow within a meeting strategic and logical? Is there connection between work the group undertakes one week to the next? Is the work connected to a larger purpose for the team and/or school? There should

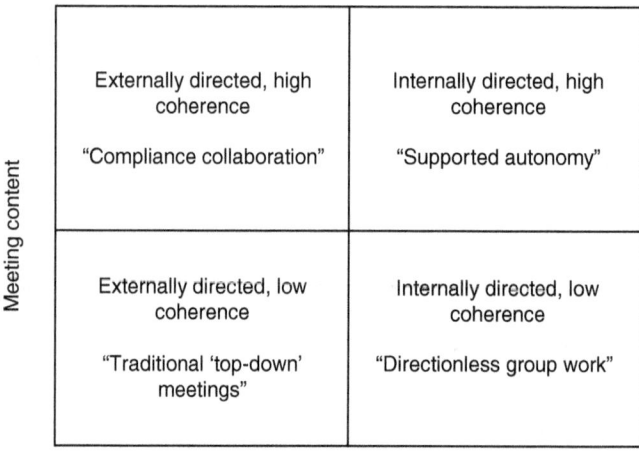

Figure 4.1 Meeting content versus teacher autonomy quadrant diagram

be a clear through line within and across meetings, so there is a consistency and larger purpose to the work of teachers across a series of meetings.

Note that we can plot our two vignette teacher groups on the diagram. The high school math data team would likely fall within the "compliance collaboration" quadrant, as the teachers have little say in what is happening, though there is likely high coherence. Dani seemed very focused on sticking to her predetermined agenda and sequence of instructional topics for the group's meetings. There is forethought and strategy, albeit somewhat misplaced. The work Dani wanted the group to accomplish—examining content standards for an upcoming unit—was solid and most likely aligned with school and district goals.

The English Language Arts team would most likely fall into the quadrant located diagonally across from the math data team: "directionless group work." The meeting began with an inquiry about what the work was supposed to be, and Tim was not even ready with the data he was supposed to bring to the meeting. Time was spent debating whether to examine the incomplete dataset, followed by noncommittal discussions about upcoming instruction. The group did not hold itself accountable to any particular outcome. Jeff, as the leader, was not much help at all, by missing most of the meeting and not assisting the team with needed communication systems, like providing an agenda ahead of the meeting, so all would know what was expected to occur. It is clear from the short vignette that expectations, generally, were not entirely clear for teachers.

As a counterpoint to the two above examples, NBRS espoused and provided examples of "supported autonomy." Teachers were the leaders of their team meetings. For example, the schools often developed leadership roles, such as facilitator or notetaker or data manager, and leaders, who were present in meetings, would be a support and source of ideas and were contributing team members, though they were not the meetings' facilitators. Further, teachers had a say (maybe not the final say, but meaningful and impactful input) in the materials their teams would purchase, what professional learning they needed, and curricular decisions. This input was the autonomy half of the construct. However, this autonomy was not left to wither, due to insufficient support. Support began with leaders creating structures and forums for teachers to express their leadership and autonomy via systems of teams and committees; holding regular meetings to discuss student progress (another forum and structure for the work to occur); and creating professional learning (and capacity building) systems like video libraries of instruction by the school's teachers, peer observations, and teachers leading professional learning experiences for their colleagues. Consider this next fictious team's work as a counterpoint to the two teams depicted in the chapter's opening vignette:

The kindergarten team at Pine Mountain Elementary School[2] entered MacKenzie's classroom for their weekly data team meeting. As the teachers entered to join MacKenzie at her kidney-shaped table, they noted, almost one after another, that their principal, Mae, was already there, greeting them as they entered. After a few moments of light and personal chatter, Stacey, the team's assigned meeting facilitator, called the meeting to order. "Hi, everyone. Did you all get the agenda for today?" Heads nodded affirmatively around the table. Indeed, they had all seen the emailed agenda Stacey had sent a few days in advance of the meeting, and they all came to the meeting prepared with their students' letter-sound data, so they could discuss their overall instructional sequence, as well as interventions for students not making adequate progress.

Team members each examined their data, and discussion ensued, with nonjudgmental comparisons, collective responsibility for all kindergarteners' performance, and offers to help develop a plan for those students not meeting expectations at that time. MacKenzie, for her part, wondered if they should create a group across their classes where one of the teachers could provide the identified students targeted practice with letter sounds a few days per week. The group really liked this idea, but they wondered about the logistics. In other words, if they were all teaching their classes, who among them could devote this time? Further, what would this magnanimous teacher leader's students do while she worked with the intervention group's students?

Silent but nonverbally engaged and focused during the meeting up until this point, Mae believed she had some ideas that could be helpful. "Well, I can give you Marcella [one of their building paraeducators] for three days during the 30-minute blocks you outlined. That way, MacKenzie can work with the intervention group, and Marcella can come in to work with the rest of the class. How would that work?"

There was nodding all around. "I think we should give it a try!" Priya enthusiastically responded, representing the nonverbal affirmation of the entire team.

"Great," continued Mae. "I will talk to Marcella this afternoon, and I will email you all when I have done so and also shuffled her schedule to free her up to help you. Also, MacKenzie, I will touch base with Regina [the reading intervention teacher at the school] to see if she has some materials you can borrow, or if she has something to suggest. I have seen her use some kits and apps on her iPad that I think would be very useful for your group." Mae started crafting an email to Regina on her laptop that very moment.

"Awesome! Thank you, Mae. That sounds great! Whatever we typically do with the group is not working for these students, so it will be great to get some ideas for how we might do this differently," Priya suggested.

After solidifying their plan for the intervention group, the team hit a lull in their momentum. Sensing the need for a nudge, Mae chimed in again. "How about your students who are in the top bands on the assessment? What might we do with them? They seem like they are ready for the next step." Without providing any more direction, Mae just listened to the subsequent conversation, nodding as the group considered pushing these students into some next-logical skills, like blending and reading some more challenging words.

The team's time came to an end, and the group exited with a general plan for the next meeting—setting up the intervention group and planning for the next skills for students who had mastered their letter sounds.

In this latest vignette, Mae displays an ideal balance of supporting her teachers and providing them autonomy—*supported autonomy*. On the support side, she began by being present in the meeting and serving as an engaged participant. Also, she provided human resource support by allocating some of a school paraeducator's time three times a week to help the kindergarten team operate their intervention idea. Further, I would add that Mae was acting supportive by endorsing ("green lighting," if you will) MacKenzie's intervention concept in the first place. Without Mae's endorsement, it is likely the plan would not come to fruition. Additionally, Mae offered to connect the team with some material support, in the form of kits and apps from the reading intervention teacher. Finally, Mae supported the team by offering a meaningful question when the team was stuck to keep them moving. Who among us has not benefited from a leader asking us a question to shake us out of a confused malaise or indecisive funk?

On the autonomy side, though Mae acted as a formal leader should in providing support, she was not the operational leader of the kindergarten team's meeting—the teacher team led their own meeting. Mae strategically monitored her "airtime," so that her contributions occurred when she had something meaningful to add and/or the group needed her help. Her participation in the meeting was strategic and checked, so her voice and ideas did not dominate. It was clear that this team was doing the kindergarten team's work, and Mae was supporting their efforts, not the other way around.

There are other important forms of support that underlie this vignette, but these are difficult to represent in one particular meeting. For example, consider that much work likely took place earlier in the school year or in past school years to build the capacity of this team to function as successfully as it does and set the expectations for data team work. For example, undoubtedly much leadership modeling, coaching, and sharing of resources helped the kindergarten team create leadership roles (i.e., MacKenzie as the facilitator, another member as the minutes taker, another as the time keeper, etc.) and operate meetings that align with the school's or district's expectations for data team work. Though the setting of expectations might, paradoxically, seem to be an erosion of autonomy (and I would agree, on the surface), this type of capacity building and setting of clear expectations, up to a point, can create a highly independent team that aims to do the work of a data team because its members see success within this work. A team that operates well does not continually need to be told to do their work because the members can intrinsically observe its value. The team will see success and want to replicate it, as this kindergarten team was certainly doing.

The preceding was an example of how supported autonomy can manifest in a teacher-led meeting situation. Next, let's consider how this construct might present in the more individual instructional role in teachers' classrooms.

Figure 4.2 displays another quadrant diagram where autonomy is crossed, in this case, with instructional support. In the upper left quadrant, teachers would experience a highly directed atmosphere, where the curriculum is scripted, and they are expected to be in a certain place on a particular day with very little opportunity for deviation. There is ample support for teachers to stick to the script. Thus, this quadrant represents the support but not the autonomy. Schools that are in a continued pattern of dysfunction and low achievement might opt for this type of model to provide some consistency of (hopefully) sound instruction for all students.

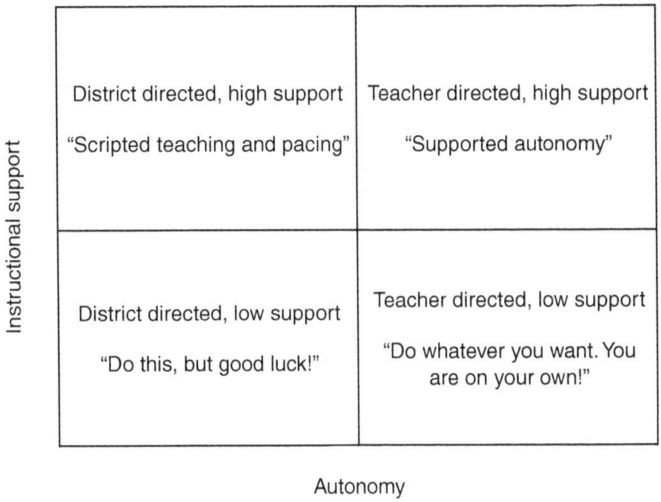

District directed, high support "Scripted teaching and pacing"	Teacher directed, high support "Supported autonomy"
District directed, low support "Do this, but good luck!"	Teacher directed, low support "Do whatever you want. You are on your own!"

(y-axis: Instructional support; x-axis: Autonomy)

Figure 4.2 Instructional support versus teacher autonomy quadrant diagram

In the lower left quadrant, teachers would similarly see a scripted scenario, where teachers are told to teach a particular way, but there is very little, if any, other support (i.e., professional learning, troubleshooting, etc.) for them. Teachers might logically come to rely on each other and the scripted program itself for support and troubleshooting. Again, due to the clear expectation of teaching a particular program or with a specific pace, there is little autonomy or decision-making for teachers.

In the lower right quadrant, teachers experience the most autonomy with little to no support. In other words, these teachers might be handed a textbook to serve as a curriculum and, due to a variety of reasons—lack of administrator capacity or time, leadership apathy, low expectations, and so on—these teachers are simply left to their own devices. So long as no problems surface, these teachers can do as they see fit. In some ways, this might seem appealing to teachers. However, given the complexity of teaching, instruction with little support, particularly for new teachers, is a recipe for mediocre results, at best.

Finally, in the upper right corner, we find the quadrant aligned with the second lesson from NBRS—supported autonomy. Here, teachers have the support they need: meaningful, ongoing, collaborative professional learning deeply connected to their daily work; appropriate and ample materials; a workable curriculum; time to collaborate; and real-time access to trusted and credible leaders and colleagues who can help them problem-solve challenges that naturally arise during the complex work of teaching students.

Part of this support is trust for the teacher as a professional, as a NBRS principal highlighted, whereby teachers are viewed as experts in instruction, and with the proper support, they will make the best decisions for their students.

Formal leaders were not the only source of support for teachers' collective autonomy. In NBRS, teachers were also—particularly during the pandemic—supported by *each other*, via colleagues' teacher leadership. The title of one of my articles about this research was "Stepping Up and Supporting Colleagues: Teacher Leadership during the COVID-19 Pandemic in US National Blue Ribbon Schools" (Visone, 2023). Teachers leaned on each other during the pandemic more than ever. At times, it was to support each other's morale and emotional well-being, via teacher appreciation events, through leading stress relief extracurricular offerings (e.g., yoga, weight loss contests, walking clubs, etc.), or simply through commiserating about common challenges. In other instances, they were supporting each other via leading colleagues' professional learning and (*particularly* during the pandemic) offering assistance with technology integration into instruction. Though much of this teacher leadership support for colleagues was addressed in the two previous chapters, it is important to understand that these teacher contributions impact supported autonomy, as well.

Thus far, in this chapter, supported autonomy has been considered through the lenses of teacher collaboration, instructional support, and peer support. Next, I provide a tool, much like the *Teacher Leadership Self-Assessment Tool for Schools* from Chapter 2 (Table 2.3), through which your school can examine supported autonomy across a variety of dimensions. An editable and printable version of this tool can be found in the Support Material collection for this book.

Table 4.2 is the *Supported Autonomy Self-Assessment Tool for Schools*. Like the analogous teacher leadership tool from Chapter 2 (Table 2.3), this tool can be used by individual educators or teams to examine the quality of supported autonomy in their schools. Detailed directions are provided on the first page of the tool, but essentially, you can use the tool like a rubric to assess the current level of supported autonomy practice in your school across a variety of specific indicators. The look-for language in the tool can help you align your school's present reality with the various proficiency levels on the tool. As with the teacher leadership tool, this tool is not designed to elicit ratings or scores. Rather, its purpose is to generate reflection and conversation that can lead to concrete and meaningful movement toward increasingly more supported autonomy for teachers.

Supported Autonomy: An Empowering Balance for Teachers' Practice

Table 4.2 Supported autonomy self-assessment tool for schools

Supported Autonomy Self-Assessment Tool for Schools

Purpose: The purpose of the *Supported Autonomy Self-Assessment Tool for Schools* is to allow educators to examine supported autonomy practice in their schools and engender dialogue about ways to maximize supported autonomy to improve school outcomes. The tool is modeled after research within U.S. National Blue Ribbon Schools (Visone, 2018, 2022, 2023). The citations for these studies are:

Visone, J. D. (2018). Developing social and decisional capital in US National Blue Ribbon Schools. *Improving Schools, 21*(2), 158–172. https://doi.org/10.1177/1365480218755171

Visone, J. D. (2022). Collaborative professionalism in US National Blue Ribbon Schools. *International Journal of Leadership in Education*, 1–22. https://doi.org/10.1080/13603124.2022.2107240

Visone, J. D. (2023). Stepping up and supporting colleagues: Teacher leadership during the COVID-19 pandemic in US National Blue Ribbon Schools. *Leadership and Policy in Schools*, 1–27. https://doi.org/10.1080/15700763.2023.2239898

Directions: Individuals or teams of educators should reflect on each row of the tool (pp. 2–6), determining which level of practice best describes the current status of supported autonomy in the school (or department, district, or other unit of analysis). You should aim to represent the holistic average of supported autonomy practice. There is no scoring necessary, as this tool is designed to generate conversation about improvement of practice, not label or quantify. In situations where there is more than one idea represented in a "look for" (e.g., from Domain I: "Administrators are viewed as trusted partners in the work, serving as respected and credible sources of support. Administrators' ideas are sought and put into action by teachers."), raters can select the column where that particular "look for" is fully realized in practice (e.g., *Limited*), while identifying specific parts of the "look for" in columns to the right, since these elements are more advanced (e.g., *Growing*).

For educator teams or individual educators, a prompt to consider for each row of the tool could be: *What best represents our school's practice?*
For individual educators, a prompt to consider for each row of the tool could be: *What best represents my own practice?*

Note that the "look for" descriptions (which are the text in each box in the three right-most columns) are organized along a spectrum of three different proficiency levels of supported autonomy practice: *limited, growing,* and *extensive*. Within a Domain, it is likely that "look fors"/rows might be rated at different levels. In other words, not all rows in the same domain need to have the same rating (column). This differential rating represents the highly contextualized nature of supported autonomy practice.

<u>How to Use This Tool</u>: Rate your school's supported autonomy practice via the tool (pp. 2–6). Once you or your team has reflected upon and rated each "look for," identify a reasonable number of "look fors" (no more than three to five, to start) that you believe are high leverage and for which you can plan action steps to move your rating farther to the right on the tool. This tool can be reexamined at regular intervals (e.g., annually) to continue your school's progress.

Supported Autonomy: An Empowering Balance for Teachers' Practice

Domain	Limited Supported Autonomy Practice	Growing Supported Autonomy Practice	Extensive Supported Autonomy Practice
I. Professional Collaboration: *Support*	___ Administrators are rarely present at formal teacher-led meetings, and when they do attend, they do not contribute significantly to the work.	___ Administrators are sometimes present at formal teacher-led meetings, and they occasionally make a meaningful contribution.	___ Administrators are consistently present at formal teacher-led meetings, offering supportive comments, asking meaningful questions, and contributing as team members.
	___ Administrators are not viewed as trusted partners in the work; they serve as sources of authority but not support. Administrators' ideas are not sought and put into action by teachers.	___ Administrators are sometimes viewed as trusted partners in the work, serving as sources of support. Administrators' ideas are infrequently sought and occasionally put into action by teachers.	___ Administrators are viewed as trusted partners in the work, serving as respected and credible sources of support. Administrators' ideas are sought and put into action by teachers.
	___ Administrators rarely provide support for teachers' work and ideas, including material, human resource, endorsement, and other supports.	___ Administrators provide some support for teachers' work and ideas, including material, human resource, endorsement, and other supports.	___ Administrators provide ongoing, real-time support for teachers' work and ideas, including material, human resource, endorsement, and other supports.
	___ Administrators do not build and maintain the capacity of teachers to collaborate, providing unclear or nonexistent expectations and little or no relevant professional learning.	___ Administrators build the capacity of teachers to collaborate, via expectations and professional learning.	___ Administrators build and maintain the capacity of teachers to collaborate autonomously and effectively, via clear expectations and ongoing professional learning.
	___ Teachers are not provided time during the school day to collaborate professionally; or, if they are, this time is during teachers' individual planning time.	___ Teachers are provided some time during the school day to collaborate professionally. This time is independent from teachers' individual planning time.	___ Teachers are provided substantial, regular, and uninterrupted time during the school day to collaborate professionally. This time is independent from teachers' individual planning time.
	___ Teachers rarely provide each other support for collaboration and, instead, look to administrators to provide support.	___ Teachers sometimes provide each other support for collaboration via troubleshooting of collaborative challenges and mostly reactive solutions.	___ Teachers regularly provide each other support for collaboration via real-time troubleshooting of collaborative challenges and proactive, strategic solutions.

Teacher Leadership Practice in High-Performing Schools

Domain	*Limited* Supported Autonomy Practice	*Growing* Supported Autonomy Practice	*Extensive* Supported Autonomy Practice
II. Professional Collaboration: *Autonomy*	__ Teachers rarely or never facilitate opportunities for professional collaboration. Administrator input is extensive. __ Administrators contribute to the team's work extensively, to the detriment of teachers' participation. Their contributions account for more than 50% of the "airtime" during typical meetings. __ Teachers do not have formal roles within their collaboration meetings, such as facilitator, minutes taker, time keeper, etc. because administrators serve in all these roles or do not build teachers' capacity to serve in these roles. __ Professional collaboration agendas are not created by teachers, as administrators direct the work of teachers during professional collaboration time.	__ Teachers facilitate some opportunities for professional collaboration with some formal administrator input. __ Administrators contribute to the team's work, but their contributions account for between 10%–50% of the "airtime" during typical meetings. __ Teachers have informal roles within their collaboration meetings, such as facilitator, minutes taker, time keeper, etc., but the roles might not be consistently active. __ Professional collaboration agendas are sometimes created by teachers. Administrators sometimes impose agenda items on the team that may or may not align with teachers' aims.	__ Teachers facilitate opportunities for professional collaboration with little to no need for formal administrator input. __ Administrators contribute to the team's work, but their contributions account for less than 10% of the "airtime" during typical meetings. __ Teachers have formal roles within their collaboration meetings, such as facilitator, minutes taker, time keeper, etc., and these roles are consistently active in meetings. __ Professional collaboration agendas are created by teachers, with possible meaningful input from administrators.

Copyright material from Jeremy D. Visone (2025), *Teacher Leadership Practice in High-Performing Schools*, Routledge

Supported Autonomy: An Empowering Balance for Teachers' Practice

III. Instruction: *Support*	___ Teachers have access to a curriculum that might be unrealistic, does not include meaningful and user-friendly resources, and does not allow teachers to make professional decisions for alterations in real time.	___ Teachers have access to a curriculum that is realistic, connected to resources, and allows teachers to make some professional decisions for alterations in real time.	___ Teachers have access to a curriculum that is realistic, connected to meaningful and user-friendly resources, and allows teachers to make professional decisions for alterations in real time.
	___ Teachers do not have access to individuals (i.e., administrators, coaches, resource teachers, colleagues, etc.) who can provide credible, ongoing, real-time, and meaningful support for teachers when questions and challenges arise. Teachers work primarily on their own.	___ Teachers have some access to individuals (i.e., administrators, coaches, resource teachers, colleagues, etc.) who can provide credible, ongoing, real-time, and meaningful support for teachers when questions and challenges arise. Teachers may not avail themselves of their assistance. They also might have access to individuals who are not helpful in this area.	___ Teachers have consistent access to a variety of individuals (i.e., administrators, coaches, resource teachers, colleagues, etc.) who can provide credible, ongoing, real-time, and meaningful support for teachers when questions and challenges arise. Teachers know of these resources and regularly avail themselves of the assistance they provide.
	___ Teachers are not provided the materials they need (i.e., supplies, texts, assessments, etc.) to effectively implement the curriculum.	___ Teachers are provided some of the materials they need (i.e., supplies, texts, assessments, etc.) to effectively implement the curriculum.	___ Teachers are provided all the materials they need (i.e., supplies, texts, assessments, etc.) to effectively implement the curriculum.
	___ Teachers are not provided with human and time-associated resources (i.e., substitute coverage, paraeducator support, time for collaboration, intervention systems, etc.) they need to effectively implement the curriculum.	___ Teachers are provided with human and time-associated resources (i.e., substitute coverage, paraeducator support, time for collaboration, intervention systems, etc.) they need to effectively implement the curriculum.	___ Teachers are provided with all the human and time-associated resources (i.e., substitute coverage, paraeducator support, time for collaboration, intervention systems, etc.) they need to effectively implement the curriculum.

Domain	Limited Supported Autonomy Practice	Growing Supported Autonomy Practice	Extensive Supported Autonomy Practice
IV. Instruction: *Autonomy*	— Teachers rarely provide support for colleagues with instructional matters. Professional learning support is generally sought from administrators.	— Teachers sometimes provide support for colleagues with instructional matters, including some, mostly reactive, solutions to challenges that arise. Professional learning support is sometimes teacher driven.	— Teachers regularly provide support for colleagues with instructional matters, including real-time and proactive solutions to challenges that arise. Professional learning support is teacher driven.
	— Teachers are not allowed to deviate from curriculum pacing and lesson expectations.	— With permission, teachers are allowed to deviate from curriculum pacing and lesson expectations, within reason, for the benefit of their students.	— Without specifically asking for permission, teachers are allowed to deviate from curriculum pacing and lesson expectations, within reason, for the benefit of their students. Teachers are trusted as professionals.
	— Teachers are told which curricular resources to use.	— Teachers have access to different curricular resources and can sometimes choose which of the resources are most appropriate for their students' needs.	— Teachers have access to many different curricular resources and can choose which of the resources are most appropriate for their students' needs.
	— Common student assessments are rarely, if ever, co-constructed with teachers' input.	— Common student assessments are sometimes co-constructed with teachers' input.	— Common student assessments are often co-constructed with teachers' input.
	— Teachers do not have the latitude to assess their students as they deem necessary.	— Beyond common assessments, teachers have some opportunity to assess their students as they deem necessary.	— Beyond common assessments, teachers have the latitude to assess their students as they deem necessary.

Supported Autonomy: An Empowering Balance for Teachers' Practice

V. Overall Supported Autonomy	___ Teachers do not frequently suggest innovations and ideas to administrators, and, when they do, their ideas are not often acted upon by administrators. Teachers are not empowered to be innovative.	___ Teachers sometimes suggest innovations and ideas to administrators, and these ideas are sometimes acted upon by administrators. Some teachers are empowered to be innovative.		___ Teachers frequently suggest innovations and ideas to administrators, and these ideas are often acted upon by administrators. Teachers are empowered to be innovative. Administrators provide teachers a "green light" culture.[3]
	___ Teachers, in many circumstances, feel compelled to ask for permission to make decisions in their day-to-day work.	___ Teachers, in some circumstances, do not feel compelled to ask for permission to make decisions in their day-to-day work.		___ Teachers, in most circumstances, do not feel compelled to ask for permission to make decisions in their day-to-day work.
	___ If asked, teachers would report that they are not treated as professionals.	___ If asked, some teachers would report that they are treated as professionals, or teachers would report that they are sometimes treated as professionals.		___ If asked, teachers would report that they are treated as professionals.
	___ If asked, teachers would report that they do not possess autonomy in their day-to-day work.	___ If asked, some teachers would report that they possess autonomy in their day-to-day work, or teachers would report that they sometimes possess autonomy in their day-to-day work.		___ If asked, teachers would report that they possess autonomy in their day-to-day work.
	___ Teachers rarely serve as a trusted source of support for the emotional well-being of their colleagues.	___ Teachers sometimes serve as a trusted source of support for the emotional well-being of their colleagues.		___ Teachers regularly and noticeably serve as a trusted source of support for the emotional well-being of their colleagues.

Summary

The second lesson from NBRS was described as *supported autonomy*. This construct was defined as: teachers at our school are provided the supports they need to effectively educate students. However, teachers are trusted by leaders to determine how to best meet students' needs. The opening vignette for the chapter displayed two teacher teams that were on either side of the supportive autonomy spectrum, with neither in balance. The first team, a high school mathematics team, had a very involved leader who was willing to provide ample structure and support to the team. However, she was not willing to provide teachers reasonable autonomy. The second team, a middle school English Language Arts team, was very autonomous. In fact, they were essentially on their own, with very little tangible support from their assigned administrator, who was not able to attend most of their meeting time.

Autonomy concerns an individual's ability to have control over their own actions. In a professional sense, greater autonomy can lead to greater connection to and positive feelings about one's organization. Society provides varying degrees of respect for different professions. For example, in the United States, doctors are afforded great respect, which is correlated with their relative autonomy in decision-making with patients. However, teachers are not afforded the same level of societal respect in the United States, as evidenced by the relatively large gap in pay between teachers and other college-educated professionals, even when compared to the analogous gaps in other developed nations. In alignment with the gap in compensation, teachers' work has not been described as autonomous in recent decades.

Other authors have previously considered the construct of autonomy for teachers. Selected findings have included that teachers were willing to trade some autonomy when adequate support was provided in curriculum implementation, that elementary teachers believed themselves to be less autonomous than secondary teachers, and that teachers generally felt that classroom management was the aspect of their work where they had the most autonomy. Other key thinkers in the profession have advocated for different forms of autonomy for teachers. For example, in collective autonomy, teachers are less bound by top-down mandates, but they are more accountable to each other. In connected autonomy, better group learning and collaboration leads to more effective autonomous work by the team's members.

In the studied NBRS, strategic structures undergirded supported autonomy. These included forums for teacher leadership and collaboration, like data teams, committees and teams, data review meetings, and representation for grade levels or departments in the work of committees and teams. Further, relational aspects of these schools' work, including trust in teachers, led to their autonomy. Teachers were trusted in these schools as professionals who were empowered to make decisions in the best interest of students. Teachers were specifically granted autonomy in such areas as collaboration, resource allocation, professional learning, and curricular decisions.

The chapter specifically examined two of the aforementioned areas where supported autonomy can be manifested in schools: teacher collaboration in teams and instruction. In a second vignette, offered as a counterexample to the two teams presented in the chapter's opening vignette, a kindergarten team was provided meaningful support by the principal during their data team meeting, while the agenda and work belonged to the teachers. The principal's support included allocating paraeducator time to help teachers operationalize an innovative intervention model across their classrooms, pointing them to specific resources that the reading intervention teacher might possess, and asking a strategic question to get the group "unstuck."

The *Supported Autonomy Self-Assessment Tool for Schools* is a rubric-like tool that teams and individual educators can use to determine the quality of supported autonomy in their school. The tool does not provide overall ratings, but rather it is a means to generate reflection and conversation that can help move a school toward increased supportive autonomy for teachers.

Questions to Consider for Chapter 4:

Supported Autonomy: An Empowering Balance for Teachers' Practice

1. In your own role as a professional educator, how much autonomy do you possess?
   a. What is tightly controlled by others?
   b. What is at your discretion?
   c. What changes would you prefer if you had the ability make changes to the present condition of autonomy?
2. In your own role as a professional educator, how much support do you receive?
   a. In what areas do you receive meaningful support, and how does this support manifest?
   b. In what areas do you not receive meaningful support?
   c. In what areas would you like to receive support for which you do not now receive it?
3. What do you think about the societal "status" of teachers and the debate about whether teaching is a profession?
4. Are elements of your school's work "loosely coupled," as Elmore has outlined? If so, how?
5. For your school, considering the quadrant diagram in Figure 4.1, how would you describe the condition of teacher collaboration in teams through the lens of supported autonomy? Are there pockets of excellence and pockets in need of focus across teams?
6. For your school, considering the quadrant diagram in Figure 4.2, how would you describe the condition of teachers' instructional choices in their classrooms through the lens of supported autonomy?

7. How would you describe the balance between support and autonomy in your school, overall? The *Supported Autonomy Self-Assessment Tool for Schools* in Table 4.2 can be useful to examine your school's work to answer this prompt.

Notes

1 Pseudonym, as are all names and places in this vignette.
2 Pseudonym, as are all names and places in this vignette.
3 Kay, K., & Boss, S. (2022). *Redefining student success: Building a new vision to transform leading, teaching, and learning*. Corwin.

References

Elmore, R. F. (2005). *School reform from the inside out: Policy, practice, and performance*. Harvard Education Press.

Elston, M. A. (1991). The politics of professional power: Medicine in a changing health service. In J. Gabe, M. Calnan, & M. Bury (Eds.), *The sociology of the health service* (pp. 58–88). Routledge.

Fullan, M. (2007). *The NEW meaning of educational change* (4th ed.). Teachers College Press.

Fullan, M. (2019). *Nuance: Why some leaders succeed and others fail*. Corwin.

Grissom, J. A., Egalite, A. J., & Lindsay, C. A. (2021). *How principals affect students and schools: A systematic synthesis of two decades of research*. The Wallace Foundation. https://cahnfellowsprograms.org/wp-content/uploads/2021/11/How-Principals-Affect-Students-and-Schools.pdf

Hargreaves, A., & O'Connor, M. T. (2018). *Collaborative professionalism: When teaching together means learning for all*. Corwin.

Hill, H. C., & Grossman, P. (2013). Learning from teacher observations: Challenges and opportunities posed by new teacher evaluation systems. *Harvard Educational Review, 83*(2), 371–384. http://meridian.allenpress.com/her/article-pdf/83/2/371/2111262/haer_83_2_d11511403715u376.pdf

Hughes, S., & Lewis, H. (2020). Tensions in current curriculum reform and the development of teachers' professional autonomy. *The Curriculum Journal, 31*(2), 290–302. https://doi.org/10.1002/curj.25

Koestner, R., & Losier, G. F. (1996). Distinguishing reactive versus reflective autonomy. *Journal of Personality, 64*(2), 465–494. https://doi.org/10.1111/j.1467-6494.1996.tb00518.x

Learning Forward. (n.d.). *Standards for professional learning*. Retrieved May 24, 2024, from https://learningforward.org/standards-for-professional-learning

Leithwood, K., Seashore Louis, K., Anderson, S., & Wahlstrom, K. (2004). *How leadership influences student learning: Review of research*. The Wallace Foundation. https://wallacefoundation.org/sites/default/files/2023-07/How-Leadership-Influences-Student-Learning.pdf

Marzano, R. J., Waters, T., & McNulty, B. A. (2005). *School leadership that works: From research to results*. ASCD.

Natanson, H. (2022, September 6). Trust in teachers is plunging amid a culture war in education. *Washington Post*. www.washingtonpost.com/education/2022/09/06/teachers-trust-history-lgbtq-culture-war/

Organization for Economic Cooperation and Development (OECD). (2021). *United States education at a glance 2021: OECD indicators*. https://doi.org/https://doi.org/10.1787/b35a14e5-en

Parchomovsky, G., & Stein, A. (2021). Autonomy. *University of Toronto Law Journal, 71*(1), 61–90. https://doi.org/10.3138/UTLJ.2019-0113

Sahlberg, P., & Walker, T. D. (2021). *In teachers we trust: The Finnish way to world-class schools*. W. W. Norton & Company.

Salvatore, D., Numerato, D., & Fattore, G. (2018). Physicians' professional autonomy and their organizational identification with their hospital. *BMC Health Services Research, 18*(1), 1–11. https://doi.org/10.1186/s12913-018-3582-z

Snedden, A. (2013). *Autonomy*. Bloomsbury.

Strong, L. E. G., & Yoshida, R. K. (2014). Teachers' autonomy in today's educational climate: Current perceptions from an acceptable instrument. *Educational Studies*, *50*(2), 123–145. https://doi.org/10.1080/00131946.2014.880922

Vangrieken, K., Grosemans, I., Dochy, F., & Kyndt, E. (2017). Teacher autonomy and collaboration: A paradox? Conceptualising and measuring teachers' autonomy and collaborative attitude. *Teaching and Teacher Education*, *67*, 302–315. https://doi.org/10.1016/j.tate.2017.06.021

Visone, J. D. (2018). Developing social and decisional capital in US National Blue Ribbon Schools. *Improving Schools*, *21*(2), 158–172. https://doi.org/10.1177/1365480218755171

Visone, J. D. (2022a). Collaborative professionalism in US National Blue Ribbon Schools. *International Journal of Leadership in Education*, 1–22. https://doi.org/10.1080/13603124.2022.2107240

Visone, J. D. (2022b). *Empowering teacher leadership: Strategies and systems to realize your school's potential*. Routledge. https://doi.org/10.4324/9781003190370

Visone, J. D. (2023). Stepping up and supporting colleagues: Teacher leadership during the COVID-19 pandemic in US National Blue Ribbon Schools. *Leadership and Policy in Schools*, 1–27. https://doi.org/10.1080/15700763.2023.2239898

Wallace Foundation. (2013). *The school principal as leader: Guiding schools to better teaching and learning*. www.wallacefoundation.org/knowledge-center/Documents/The-School-Principal-as-Leader-Guiding-Schools-to-Better-Teaching-and-Learning-2nd-Ed.pdf

Collaborative Professionalism for Teams' Work

"Our students are always really confused by the cause of seasons," noted Nick,[1] the team leader for the Greenwood Middle School Grade 8 science team. The group consisted of three science teachers, one for each team of students. The team was about to begin a unit of study on Earth's place within the solar system. The unit would cover, along with the seasons, tides, phases of the moon, and planetary orbits, among other Earth and space science topics. "I want us to devise a better method of helping students understand this difficult, abstract concept," he added.

"Agreed," stated Mira, nodding affirmatively. Sheila, the last of the science teachers, was also nodding with approval.

"Let's see if we can teach this in a more interactive way," Nick suggested. Fingers were rapidly typing on laptop keyboards as the team attempted to find inspiration online.

"Sorry I am late!" Jamal noted, hustling into a seat, still a bit out of breath from jogging to the meeting from across the building. Jamal was the building's assistant principal, and he was the administrative liaison for the team.

"No worries, Jamal," Mira responded. "You have not missed much, yet. We have just determined that we want to teach the seasons in a more interactive manner, so our students will understand this concept better."

Jamal indicated that he liked the sound of a more interactive approach. "Please let me know what I might be able to do to help. For example, if you need any materials ... "

The group thanked Jamal for his espoused support and continued their independent searching for ideas. After a few minutes, Sheila broke the silence. "We know that NGSS [Next Generation Science Standards] call for students to use models. Why don't we have the kids create models that they can use to convince others of the mechanism behind the seasons? We could let them choose their approach. Like, they could work in groups to create a 3D model with clay that shows Earth's tilt in relation to its orbit around the sun, or they could draw a diagram that shows the angle of the sun's rays, or they could create an explanatory video using a heat and light source—like a heat lamp—and thermometers at various angles in relation to the lamp."

"That is a great idea, Sheila," Mira commented. "We had that model assignment that we used for weathering and erosion earlier in the year. We could start with that document and just splice in the new content."

"OK," Nick shared, "I have that document here. I can just make a copy and share it up on the screen, and we can tweak it as we need to."

The group used their time at the meeting to create an interactive model experience for students that all teachers would use in their separate classrooms. Jamal did not talk much, but when he did, he offered helpful suggestions and connections. For example, he reminded the group that the library media center and technology labs both had some video editing equipment that students could use to create or edit their videos. He also noted that there was an interdisciplinary connection to math, with angles of the sun's rays striking Earth's surface. Upon making this connection, Sheila asked if Jamal could speak to the school's math coach, Eliza, to inquire about any helpful materials that she might have to offer. Jamal wrote her an email as the team continued to work. By the end of the meeting, Jamal had forwarded a set of potential resources and connections from Eliza, including an infographic about the math behind the seasons, with graphs plotting the sun's angle in the sky versus average daily temperature and comparing average daily temperature by date between Earth's two hemispheres.

"It might be nice if we had a model or two to show the students, so they could have some inspiration," Mira suggested. "Sheila, you are very design talented—perhaps you can create something like that. I will take our rubric from the weathering and erosion project and convert it to this assignment, while Nick continues working on the description packet."

Sheila blushed a bit. "Sure. I can work on that. I will reach out to Gina [the school's technology teacher] and Jose [the school's art teacher] to see if they have any ideas that can make my creation more impactful—and aesthetically pleasing!"

With about five minutes remaining in their time together, Sheila called the group back together to review their "homework" assignments between this meeting and the next week's. In addition, they discussed an agenda for the next meeting, where they wanted to examine the results of a common formative assessment they were about to administer. Sheila captured a quick summary of the group's work on a chronological agenda and minutes document, while adding the bulleted agenda items for the next meeting. "I want to be respectful of everyone's time. I think this is a good stopping point for today."

Jamal congratulated the group on a highly productive meeting and a solid plan to increase the levels of student engagement with and understanding of an abstract and traditionally challenging concept.

The Grade 8 science team in the vignette above exemplifies many attributes of effective collaborative groups. There was clear leadership, both in the form of internal teacher leadership, with Nick providing his team with purpose and focus, and Sheila providing structure, timekeeping, and recordkeeping, and formal administrative support, with Jamal offering relevant ideas and following through on offers to gather outside resources. Though Jamal was an engaged and materially helpful participant, the teachers ran their own meeting, and they would have been self-sufficient should Jamal have been pulled away from the group to deal with an urgent matter. The group made logical connections to other professionals and their expertise throughout the school. The group did not bicker or debate or waste time about unimportant or territorial matters. They just dove in and did what needed to be done, without complaint. Ultimately, the group worked together to create experiences for their students to ensure that all students, not just the ones in their own, individual classrooms, would be successful.

As a former school principal, this vignette reminds me of so many of the most effective and cohesive teams in buildings where I worked. These were the teams that saw the best, most consistent results. Teams such as these exhibit many qualities within a framework that Hargreaves and O'Connor (2018a) refer to as *collaborative professionalism*, a construct that was introduced briefly in Chapter 4. Perhaps this team resembled your own team or a team at your school. If so, be encouraged, as research suggests these types of collaboration are impactful for student outcomes. Further, this type of collaboration also leads to the final key lesson from my research with U.S. National Blue Ribbon Schools (NBRS). Namely, these teachers

Table 5.1 The third key lesson about teacher leadership practice in National Blue Ribbon Schools

collaborative ethos and systems	Educators across roles, particularly teachers, do not work in isolation. Educators at our school learn, solve problems, plan, and innovate collaboratively.

displayed a collaborative ethos and worked within collaborative systems. Walls of traditional teacher isolation were overcome with collective work. Teachers learned, solved problems, planned, and innovated together. It should also be noted that this collaborative work was not limited to teams of teachers only. Their administrators, instructional coaches, resource teachers, related service personnel, and many other adults enhanced the collaboration. The final key lesson is shown in Table 5.1.

Due to the alignment between the final key lesson and the collaborative professionalism framework, we will examine this framework for teachers' teamwork. However, before we do that, we will consider a quick geological analogy for the traditional school.

The Traditional Challenge for Schools: The School as an Archipelago

An *archipelago* is a chain of islands that are often formed by similar circumstances. These islands can be close to a continental mainland, such as the many islands near Finland, or be rather remote and isolated within a vast expanse of ocean, such as the Hawaiian Islands. Scientists interested in biology and evolution are drawn to study organisms living on archipelagos, as these environments provide some degree of isolation from mainland biological activity and, oftentimes, depending on the ability for species to travel, even from the other archipelago's islands themselves (Shaw & Gillespie, 2016). Further, these habitats were frequently much more recently created in terms of geological time. Thus, the spread of species and their ability to evolve in the short history of these islands is of particular interest. The spread of these species is often related to relative proximity. In other words, species tend to spread from one island to the next nearest one, and the relative age of the island typically predicts how much spread can have occurred there, with the most recently added islands being the least diverse in terms of species spread. Also interesting is the progression of species movement in a predictable pattern in situations where an archipelago is formed by a geological hot spot. This is when there is a break in Earth's surface in the middle of one of Earth's tectonic plates that allows escaping lava to form an island chain. Since tectonic plates regularly and linearly slide over the surface of hot spots, which remain stationary, the island chain, such as the Hawaiian archipelago, is formed in a sequential, relatively straight line (National Oceanic and Atmospheric Administration, n.d.).

Archipelago islands are connected by many factors, such as method of formation, general geographic area, relative geological age, as well as other human characteristics (if the islands are inhabited), such as language, national association, religion, and so on. However, the individual islands' relative isolation from each other leads to elements that are unique to each island, particularly in cases where islands are spread apart from each other. Distinctive features that vary by island might include societal elements such as unique cultures, customs, ethnic makeups, and so forth. (Bräuchler, 2017). It is within this latter situation that we can find a useful analogy for schools, where each classroom might be connected to adjacent ones by common school goals; administration; general community support; funding; and, if at the secondary level, even its students. However, what happens within each individual classroom is very much its own culture and climate.

Naturally, this individuality within classrooms exists for a variety of reasons. There is the obvious individuality of the teachers who lead each classroom. This is a wonderful trait of our education system, that children are taught by creative and individual human beings who can bring their diversity of experiences, knowledge bases, and ideas to create learning experiences that can inspire and maintain student interest from one room to the next. Fortunately, our system is not one of robotic or mechanized instructional delivery—*at least not yet*, despite the proliferation of artificial intelligence—and I will most certainly not advocate for a completely homogenized approach in this work. However, from a curricular and pedagogical perspective, it would benefit our profession if we did not hear from teachers that they are isolated from their peers' instruction, though they might literally be teaching in the classroom next door. The profession would benefit by teachers having the opportunity to learn from and with each other, for the improvement of individual teacher practice, and, by extension, of student outcomes (Hargreaves & O'Connor, 2018a, 2018b; Ross, 2013).

Consider some of what my colleague Dr. Bethany Mather and I found when we asked teachers about a peer observation system in their schools (Mather & Visone, 2024b). In brief, these teachers had experienced *collegial visits*, a system for professional learning whereby teachers learn from watching each other teach. In this particular model of peer observation, foci for visits are teacher determined; visits to classrooms are for a full lesson; and, most importantly, all participants, including the host teachers, debrief shortly after the visit, so real-time feedback, two-way dialogue, and next steps can be considered by all (Visone, 2016). In our recent research about collegial visits, and relevant to this discussion about the analogy of the school-as-archipelago, teachers shared with us what their professional life was like before collegial visits were implemented. In other words, they offered a glimpse into what the professional culture resembled prior to teachers being comfortable with visiting their peers' classrooms and hosting visitors in their own rooms. Teachers used words like "island," "isolated," and "cave" to describe their own classrooms, emphasizing that they viewed this seclusion as detrimental to their growth as teachers and pedagogy. They further noted that they should move away from this situation and work together more—vacate these islands, so to speak—in order to be more effective (Mather & Visone, 2024b). We couldn't agree more.

Fortunately for these teachers, they had the opportunity to experience collegial visits, which they shared with us created a culture of *deisolation*. A particular teacher exemplified the cultural shift by explaining that, prior to seeing colleagues' instruction via collegial visits, she felt alone to figure out her curriculum, but collegial visits helped her to no longer feel alone. Further, experiences of observing colleagues' teaching in a systematic manner also increased teachers' individual *self-efficacy* (Mather & Visone, 2024b), which is a teacher's belief that they can positively impact student outcomes (Tschannen-Moran et al., 1998), *and* their *collective teacher efficacy* (Mather & Visone, 2024a), which is the belief of a group of educators that they can *collectively* affect student outcomes in a positive way (Goddard et al., 2000). Both of these constructs are known to our profession as key predictors for student success (Goddard et al., 2000; Hargreaves & O'Connor, 2018a; Hattie & Anderman, 2019; Ross, 2013; Tschannen-Moran et al., 1998), so understanding ways to improve them is valuable to schools.

This particular example of teacher collaborative work brings us back to the original analogy. Do we want our schools to behave like archipelagos? My answer is more nuanced than a simple "yes" or "no." On the one hand, teacher individuality and ability to inspire students with their creativity and genuinely unique classroom cultures are so important and valued in effective schools. This was no different in the studied NBRS. Further, teachers need to have discretion to make individualized decisions in the best interest of their students (see *supported autonomy* in Chapter 4). There are likely hundreds of such micro decisions that teachers must make every day, such as what feedback to provide students (i.e., What is the next and most important step for this student, based upon where the student's work stands right now?); whether to move ahead to the next curricular topic versus spending more time on a challenging concept that is proving difficult to some students; how to handle a particular disciplinary situation, given a student's history and nature of the offense; and so on. The ability for teachers to use what they have learned on their own and with the help of their colleagues to make the best decisions for students is known as *decisional capital* (Hargreaves & Fullan, 2012). Thus, each teacher, in the small moments in their individual classrooms, should have the flexibility and confidence to make individual decisions on behalf of their students. This is an argument on the "pro" side of the archipelago debate.

On the other hand, there is also great value in the power of collaborative work, as we will see next via a useful framework and, shortly after that, from my findings from NBRS. As to the latter, I will again make the connection between the finding of these collaborative practices in NBRS and these schools' track record for student success when these practices were found to be in operation. Teachers can do wonderful work in isolation and, in so many cases of toxic cultures, *in spite of* their overall climates, leaders, and colleagues. However, to achieve greatness across a school at scale, this individualized, isolated (imagine a single island within the archipelago analogy here) approach will not suffice.

Collective Work to the Rescue!

The nature of collaborative work in schools has been investigated by many researchers in our field, but a particularly helpful framework, and one that aligns with my findings in NBRS, comes from Andy Hargreaves and Michael O'Connor (2018a) and is known as *collaborative professionalism*.

For their research, they studied five different collaborative education efforts from around the world. These efforts included lesson study groups in a Hong Kong secondary school; collections of rural schools in the United States, Colombia, and Canada; and a particular elementary school in Norway. From these diverse settings and purposes, the authors were able to draw out commonalities related to the schools' successes.

Within this framework, the authors outlined 10 tenets. First is *collective autonomy* (note that this construct was introduced in Chapter 4), which, to review quickly, refers to a condition where the accountability is found more within the group of teachers than from administrators. Second is *collective efficacy*, which was defined above as the belief by a group of educators that they can positively affect student outcomes and is strongly and positively correlated with student achievement. Third is *collaborative inquiry*, where teachers work together to examine thoroughly and then solve problems of practice. Fourth is *collective responsibility*, which means that *all* students in the school are the concern of *all* educators, not just students' individual teachers, and educators are obligated to help one another. Fifth is *collective initiative*, which is about the group not waiting to be told what to do by formal leaders and manifests the commitment of teachers to initiate action. Sixth is *mutual dialogue*, which refers to quality conversations characterized by their depth that collaboratively professional groups undertake, including providing honest feedback, disagreeing respectfully, and having difficult conversations when needed. Seventh is *joint work*, which can certainly include teachers undertaking curricular, assessment, and pedagogical tasks together, such as illustrated in this chapter's opening vignette. Eighth is *common meaning and purpose*, which implies that all on the team are moving in the same direction and aim for ideals that transcend mere test scores and address the needs of the whole student. Ninth is *collaborating with students*, which is fairly self-explanatory, but requires a rejection of the traditional, hierarchical, power-heavy relationship imbalance between teachers and students. Finally, the 10th tenet is *big-picture thinking for all*, which I relate to systems thinking, a construct that will occupy a good portion of this chapter's pages.

This framework was very useful in examining the work of the highly successful NBRS. Without great surprise, if you have been paying attention to this book's messages, I found considerable alignment between NBRS' practices (Visone, 2018, 2022a) and various tenets of collaborative professionalism, as outlined by Hargreaves and O'Connor (2018a). These connections are outlined next.

A logical place to begin this analysis is within the realm of beliefs. Namely, the collective responsibility of the framework was manifested through statements involving "we" versus "I." For example, an elementary school noted in their application that all the school's children "belong" to all the educators, as opposed to individual teachers (Visone, 2018). Several teacher leaders explained that they make no excuses and understand their job is to ensure all students are safe and work together with their colleagues to do what is best for the students (Visone, 2022a).

Relatedly, the collaborative inquiry and joint work elements of the framework were well represented, and these were an antidote to traditional isolation. (Recall the earlier discussion about islands.) For example, an elementary principal explained, after noting the urgency she felt in an isolated culture in the school's recent past, how teachers came to understand their role in a deisolated culture in a progression from what teachers do in their own classrooms, to how that impacts what is done at the grade level, and finally to the first two levels' impact on the work of the entire school. This progression also connects to the big-picture thinking element of the framework, as teachers can see how their individual contributions connect to a larger, coherent whole. Another principal offered a more practical motivation for the shift to collaborative work for teachers—*time*, noting that teachers who function as islands simply cannot get all their work done well (Visone, 2022a).

The most prevalent manifestation of the collaborative inquiry and joint work elements of the framework were through the category of learning with and from each other. Professional learning in NBRS took many forms, some traditional and others less so. For example, in a more traditional sense, teachers learned through professional learning workshops, book studies, and via their more experienced colleagues. From the perspective of teacher leadership, these opportunities were often facilitated by teachers rather than administrators and outside consultants (Visone, 2018, 2022a).

In addition, teachers in NBRS learned from each other in many non-traditional ways, as well, and these included sharing lessons plans; sharing materials; participating in cross-disciplinary or vertical exchanges and teams; and engaging in virtual collaborations, including creating electronic repositories for resources (Visone, 2018, 2022a). Further, peer observations were mentioned across many schools, and, as noted earlier in this chapter, collegial visits (a specific form of peer observation) have been shown to impact teachers' self-efficacy and collective teacher efficacy (Mather & Visone, 2024a, 2024b), the latter of which, you will recall, is another tenet of collaborative professionalism. One school shared on their application that teachers used walk-throughs as mechanisms for learning, support, and praise (Visone, 2018). A principal outlined how the school leveraged peer observations, providing details about an observation form visiting teachers use to capture what they saw and what they want to discuss more with their colleagues. A teacher leader shared that a teaching colleague is always welcome to and often does visit her classroom to observe how the teacher leader runs her stations and guided reading in a workshop model. She further added that this offer is extended to any teacher (Visone, 2022a). I have found that such learning from observing peers' instruction can increase *social capital* (Visone, 2022b), which equates to quality collaboration and professional relationships among teachers (Hargreaves & Fullan, 2012), as well as positively impact the quality of teachers' instructional practices, as measured by administrator walk-throughs (Visone, 2022b).

Joint work also includes, *well* ... doing work *together*. According to Hargeaves and O'Connor (2018a), doing work together is the crux of true and effective collaboration, which should not be limited to collegial sharing and reflection, with the latter set of practices being more passive and less likely to lead to action or changes in practice. Without overcomplicating things, the traditional isolation of teachers in their practice leaves teachers wrestling with the same problems in their own classrooms, independently, resulting in a very uneven pattern of success across a given school (Elmore, 2000, 2005). This is a challenge of scale, meaning that not every child will receive the benefit of all the knowledge individual teachers have developed through their experience and professional learning. However, by bringing teachers together to learn with and from each other, as noted above, the capacity of a group of teachers increases, and gaps in instructional skill begin to diminish across teachers. In NBRS, joint work was commonly cited as a strength and integral to their success.

Through collaborative groups, such as professional learning communities, data teams, grade-level teams, and other configurations, these schools described how teachers regularly examined problems of practice together, leveraged student data to drive instruction, planned units and lessons together, taught lessons together, and otherwise conducted their business collaboratively. Many schools specifically espoused their affinity for collaboration and teamwork, as well as the importance of these characteristics to their success (Visone, 2018, 2022a).

Likely because of the frequent and pervasive collective work, my research did not find traditional walls of isolation in NBRS. A teacher leader explained how teachers are willing to help each other out, as opposed to an environment where teachers close their classroom doors. Another teacher addressed the traditional challenge of scale by noting that an important benefit of teachers' joint work is that, via team planning, teachers can pace the curriculum together. In this way, a principal noted, children across the school can receive an equitable and consistent experience (Visone, 2022a).

A final connection to the collaborative professionalism framework in NBRS, collective initiative, was summed up perfectly by a principal, who noted that her teachers find out what needs to be done and then they do it, without complaining about their contractual language. Teachers were not waiting for instructions from administrators, nor were they wasting time bickering about what their job was and was not. There was a pattern of teachers doing and going beyond expectations to do so (Visone, 2022a).

Overall, there was great representation of the collaborative professionalism framework tenets evident in NBRS. Further, it should be noted that Hargreaves and O'Connor (2018a) also shared the importance of trust of and support for teachers to allow collaborative professionalism to take root. These elements were described previously in Chapter 4, within the context of supported autonomy and collective autonomy. The only element in Hargreaves and O'Connor's framework that was not specifically found in my research with NBRS was collaborating with students. However, as my research was more concerned with interactions among adults, it is likely that such practices with students were not found simply because they were not sought. I would be willing to bet that these schools did collaborate with students to some degree.

At this point, you understand what tenets comprise collaborative professionalism and how teams of teachers, particularly those led by teacher leaders, in NBRS exhibited these characteristics. Next, we will examine the practical side of moving your school toward collaborative professionalism. As noted earlier, we will focus heavily on the tenet of "big-picture thinking." This aspect of collaborative professionalism was not found with great regularity in my research. Of course, this does not mean that teachers in these schools lacked this perspective, but they and their administrators did not highlight this type of thinking as integral to their success. Given the lack of emphasis, and understanding this tenet's importance within collaborative professionalism, I will devote attention here to helping teachers see the big picture and understand the system better. I know from working with my own students—teachers who are aspiring leaders—that they greatly value our work with systems thinking. These are perspectives teachers have not typically learned before they arrive at our administrator preparation program, and they immediately recognize the value of these perspectives and make connections to their own schools' successes and shortcomings.

Helping Our Staff "See in Systems"

As noted above, one of the tenets of collaborative professionalism is big-picture thinking. To help teachers, particularly teacher leaders, whose practice is the focus of this book, gain meaningful big-picture thinking, I recommend an understanding of systems, more specifically, their own schools as systems.

Schools are complex systems that exist within a larger, even more complex system (Shaked & Schechter, 2020). It is more than understandable that teachers, who are consumed with the day-to-day operations of their classrooms, managing student needs, planning lessons, correcting student work, and supervising children for the vast majority of their fast-paced days, would not possess a great understanding of systems that exist outside their classrooms. However, for teacher leaders to impact their schools beyond those classrooms in meaningful ways, gaining a systems perspective is valuable.

Naturally, this single section of one chapter in a solitary book will not be able to capture the enormity of systems thinking for teacher leaders. Rather, I will share some selected aspects of systems thinking in schools that are useful for teachers when applying leadership skills in service to their schools and colleagues. Some respected thinkers in our field have articulated key aspects of systems thinking, and I will next share a few of these thinkers' insights, which represent some of my favorites for my own aspiring leader students.

First, Bolman and Deal (2017) provided a framework for understanding complex organizations, like schools, and changes that occur within them.

Their model includes fours frames, or lenses, through which problems can be understood. These frames are the structural, human resource, political, and symbolic. The structural frame includes the rules, procedures, protocols, hierarchies, and other established guiding principles of the school. Within this frame, teacher leaders, when attempting to lead change in their buildings, might consider questions such as:

- What rule, policy, or protocol governs this challenge, and which of these might need to change?
- Whose permission might be needed?
- How does communication flow (or not) relate to this challenge?
- How does this potential change align with our goals, vision, mission, and so on?

The human resource frame is concerned with the people in the system—children, families, educators, and other staff members. Here, teacher leaders might ask:

- Who is and is not being served well by the system as it is presently designed?
- What do various groups and individuals need?
- How can leadership meet the needs of various groups and individuals?
- Who will be affected by proposed changes?

The political frame is related to competing interests, alliances, competition, and other causes of interpersonal conflict. Teacher leaders might consider such questions as:

- Whose support should we seek early in the process?
- What motivates this individual or group?
- What common interests can we find?

Finally, the symbolic frame deals with what lies under the surface of actions within the school. For example, a popular tradition in the school is beloved, and its value to the school community transcends what actually transpires at the event. Its symbolic meaning is more powerful than the event itself. Teacher leaders might consider such questions as:

- To whom is this important, and why? Conversely, to whom is this unimportant, and why?
- What myths about our school exist, and what purpose do they serve?
- What symbolic practices could help our school with this particular challenge?

The four frames provide teacher leaders with many ideas for attacking problems.

Another often-referenced, research-based framework in education is the Concerns-Based Adoption Model (Hall & Hord, 2019). This model includes multiple frames of reference for examining the change process in schools. In particular, I will focus here on Stages of Concern, which relate to how individuals feel about changes they are being asked to incorporate into their practice. The stages range from the lowest level of *unconcerned*, where a teacher does not even want to know about possible changes, to the highest level of *refocusing*, where a teacher is so deeply interested in a change process that the teacher is working to improve it. An important stage in the middle of the framework is the *personal concerns* stage, where a teacher is concerned with how the change will affect the individual personally, and less so about how the change might affect others. It is a very egocentric stage, and we can likely all picture in our mind's eye colleagues (perhaps, even ourselves!) exclaiming a list of proposed grievances against a change process. *How am I going to make this work? Why do I have to do this? I thought I knew what I was doing! Now, it will be like starting all over again! I might not feel confident in my abilities, again.* Another stage from the middle of the framework is the *management concerns* phase, where a teacher now understands why the change needs to occur but does not understand how to do what is being asked.

The power of the Stages of Concern framework is how it can help leaders (both formal and teacher leaders) see what individuals in their midst need in order to move forward. For example, teachers stuck in the personal concerns stage need to hear messages from their leaders such as: *we are going to learn this together; none of us is the expert, just yet; we will figure this out together; you do not need to have this change figured out by tomorrow—we have a plan that will allow us all to learn what we need to over time; you will have the support you need;* and so on. Conversely, teachers who are stuck at the management concerns stage are already feeling the cultural support they need. However, these teachers need the logistics. They need to know *how* to do it. For example, these teachers would benefit from going to observe a colleague who has it figured out. They would appreciate a screenshot manual. They want to work with the instructional coach or resource teacher to learn the "how to." Responses to colleagues stuck in various stages of concern are important leadership moves to help these teachers move forward.

Another valuable framework concerns a construct Heifetz et al. (2009) from the Harvard Business School call *adaptive leadership*. The authors point out that adaptive challenges, which I will note represent so many of the problems facing educators in schools, are only properly addressed through changing individuals' priorities, beliefs, habits, loyalties, and so forth. This construct directly connects to the Stages of Concern of Hall and Hord (2019), and the four frames of Bolman and Deal (2017), because we need to tap into how teachers feel and what they believe to be important. It is not enough to change the conditions, such as the curriculum, the schedule, the budget, and so on. We are working with people in a very human business. If we want to lead people, we need to convince them to come along with us and work alongside us, rather than just tell them what to do, even if what we are recommending is compelling and likely effective.

Heifetz et al. (2009) added that old ways of knowing and doing must be abandoned to address adaptive challenges. Experimentation (including a toleration for failure along the way), diverse viewpoints (rather than just the traditional few leaders), and dedicated time for change to occur (as opposed to *yesterday* or *as soon as possible*!) are all key elements of leading for adaptive change. Another key principle of Heifetz et al.'s (2009) model is that organizations, like schools or school districts, are functioning in ways that please their members to some degree. Rather than seeing a school as "broken" or "dysfunctional," those who wish to improve matters need to diagnose what is leading the school to behave the way it does. Change is not happening because the school does not want to change.

Interestingly, on the psychological level, the authors assert that people do not necessarily resist change by itself; rather, they resist perceived potential personal losses that might result from changes. (Recall the personal concerns stage of Hall and Hord [2019].) Thus, the work of those leading change is to anticipate and address potential perceived losses to create buy-in for change.

Heifetz et al. (2009) also framed adaptive change from the perspective of disequilibrium. Much like educators use Vygotsky's *Zone of Proximal Development* (1978) as the "sweet spot" for learning that is just beyond the reach of the learner, where a learner can push beyond their present capacity with assistance of teachers or more-capable peers, Heifetz et al. discussed the *Productive Zone of Disequilibrium*, where leaders push others out of their comfort zone just enough to garner attention for the change and move things forward, but not so far as to cause irreparable damage and lasting harm to the organization. Naturally, in schools, one of the key drivers of this type of disequilibrium is the examination of data to engender conversation and impetus for change. For example, *why is a particular subgroup of our students consistently not performing? Are we as a group (i.e., grade level, department, school, etc.) OK with this?* Leadership questions like these can push a group into productive disequilibrium.

Naturally, once momentum is created for change, learning needs to occur. Whether that is learning focused on understanding the problem or on potential solutions, tenets of collaborative professionalism are invaluable to maximizing a group's learning. A final, helpful systems-related framework I will share before we examine how schools can apply their knowledge of systems relates to levels of learning, first proposed by an engineer, Douglas Englebart, at a technology conference in 1968 (cited in Bryk et al., 2015). As Bryk et al. then applied this framework to schools, *Level A* learning is what individual educators learn on their own and through experiences in their own classrooms. Obviously, this first level of learning is important so that teachers are equipped to make daily decisions in their classrooms. However, Level A learning will only bring a collective group so far, and without some sharing and collective learning, inconsistencies across classrooms noted earlier (see Elmore, 2005) will be profound.

Level B learning involves what teachers and other educators can learn from each other in a workspace. This type of learning occurs through many of the tenets of collaborative professionalism, such as collaborative inquiry, joint work, mutual dialogue, collective initiative, big-picture thinking, and the collaboration that occurs within the condition of collective autonomy, among others (Hargreaves & O'Connor, 2018a). Imagine that this learning occurs within a school's teams. It is intra-team learning. This level of learning is critical to schools' success, and it was a key finding about collaboration within NBRS.

However, there is a level of learning *beyond* Level B that incorporates a systems approach—*Level C*. In this highest order of learning, the exchange of ideas goes beyond the usual teams or groups of teachers, and it may even extend beyond the school. These are inter-team learning opportunities. Consider, for example, interdepartmental or vertical grade-level sharing. Consider schools learning by collaborating with other schools. Perhaps teachers go to another school to observe and learn about their practices. Or teachers attend a conference for their subject area and return to the school with new ideas to share with colleagues. This level of learning promotes an exchange of ideas in the most powerful way since it capitalizes on preexisting Levels A and B learning. Level C learning has a multiplicative effect.

The preceding, brief outline of a few useful frames of reference for teacher leaders in understanding the "big picture" of their schools and systems thinking was provided as a preface to how teacher leaders can apply these ideas in their own work. Recall this book's focus is teacher leadership. With teachers acquiring a big-picture understanding via collaborative work to understand challenges and systems around them, as advocated for teachers by Hargreaves and O'Connor (2018a), teacher leaders can more articulately (and strategically!) advocate for their students' and colleagues' needs, as well as help lead work to alter these systems in a productive manner. Next, we will consider practical means for all educators, including teacher leaders, to use systems-thinking principles in their collaborative work.

When problem-solving, it is helpful for teacher leaders to "see" the systems within which they work, and many authors have offered means to do so. A particular favorite of mine is the fishbone diagram, applied usefully to education by Bryk et al. (2015). However, I will not repeat others' efforts here; rather, I will present a few new tools for unpacking systems.

There is no single right approach or tool, and educators should choose what works best for them. Note that the tools I will share can be useful for Level B teams, such as individual grade-level or departmental teams. However, teacher leaders are members of many Level C teams across their schools and districts as well, such as school leadership teams, district improvement teams, early intervention teams, attendance teams, school- and district-wide data teams, and so on. Thus, the tools I will share can be thought of as applicable to myriad different teams that include educators in various roles within a school or district.

The first tool borrows from my education for my first career, as a physical therapist. I spent a lot of time in physics classes, where the use of "free body" diagrams was useful to understand the forces acting upon a particular object. In physics classrooms, such forces included friction, gravitational pull, magnetic attraction, contact with another object in motion, and so forth. For our purposes, the *Free Body Diagram for Systems Thinking Tool* allows teacher teams to situate whatever they are examining (i.e., a problem of practice, a proposed change, etc.) amid the many systems-based inputs, outputs, and other considerations that they need to examine before taking action. Users of the tool could consider the systems-thinking frames referenced above (recall, for example, Bolman & Deal, 2017; Bryk et al., 2015; Hall & Hord, 2019; Heifetz et al., 2009), as well as any other systems-based approaches they have learned, to thoroughly understand their chosen issue before taking action (Heifetz et al., 2009). You can find the tool in Figure 5.1. Note that an editable and printable version of the tool can be found in the Support Material collection for this book.

It is important to note that this tool is designed to be customizable. For the sake of starting somewhere, I included three bubbles for input considerations, three for output considerations, and two bubbles to be used with a consideration of any other factors that might not fit neatly into the input and output categories. Teams or individuals using this tool can reconfigure the bubbles' purposes, add bubbles, or take some bubbles away, without believing that they did something "incorrectly." As with most tools I am sharing, this one is not for aesthetics or polished presentation. It is a tool to inspire thinking, conversation, understanding of systems, and, eventually, action. Thus, this tool can be easily recreated on a chart paper or dry-erase board.

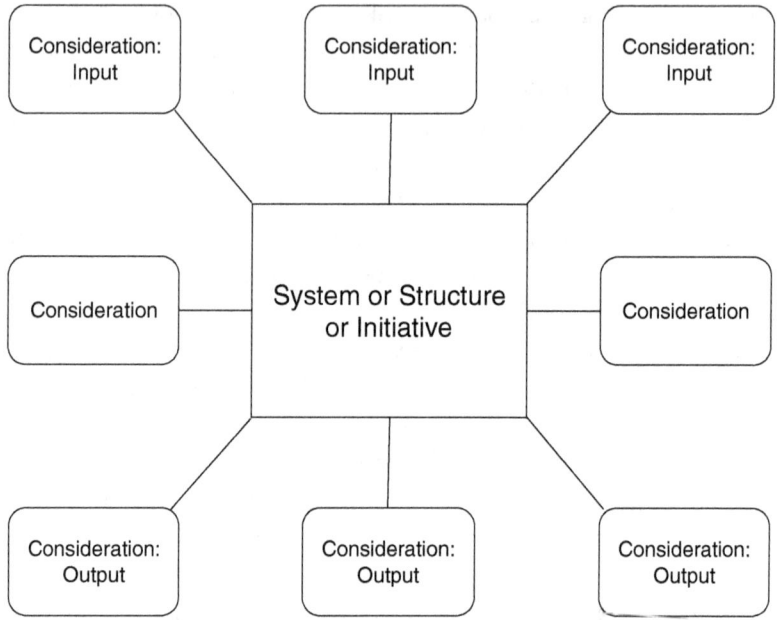

Considerations could include:

    Communications, schedules, human resources, budgetary concerns, causes, effects, etc.

Inputs are causes or other considerations that will impact the system, structure, or initiative.

Outputs are effects or other considerations that will be impacted by the system, structure, or initiative.

<u>Note</u>: There is no set number of outer "consideration" bubbles needed, so long as the system, structure, or initiative is thoroughly examined and considered. This applies to the input and output bubbles as well. Use as many as you need, either deleting or adding as necessary.

Figure 5.1 Free body diagram for systems thinking tool

In the tool, *considerations* are any systems-related factors that might influence the issue or initiative the team is studying. Such considerations might include communications, schedules, human resources, budgetary concerns, causes, effects, and so on. Inputs are factors that can have an impact on the chosen focus. Outputs are potential effects or outcomes based upon the impact of the chosen focus. For example, please find a sample, completed tool about a school-wide intervention model in

Collaborative Professionalism for Teams' Work

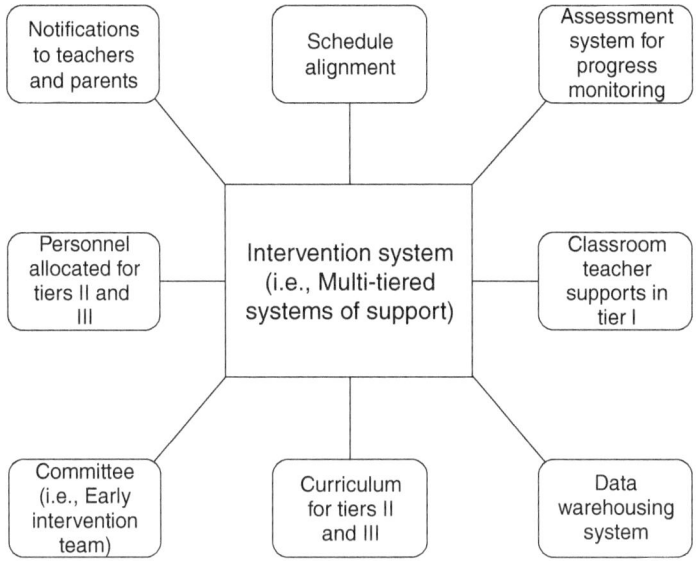

Figure 5.1 (Continued)

the continuation of Figure 5.1. As another example, for a math department examining teacher recommendations to students for math course enrollments for the following year, based upon the department's own dissatisfaction with the current model, input considerations could include parental requests and feedback, availability of student assessment results, student requests and feedback, school counseling staff knowledge of available courses and recommendations, administrative approval, and sequencing articulated by the school's course catalog. Output factors might include the final course selections by students, how students perform in their courses in subsequent years and how this performance correlates with teacher recommendations, how ratings are consistent across math teachers, and student reactions to these recommendations. Other considerations that are neither input nor output per se might include the timing of recommendations to students, community culture with parental overrides of teacher placement recommendations, and how other subjects handle the recommendations.

To make a few connections to the systems-thinking frameworks noted above, consideration about how other subject-area teachers complete their recommendations is an example of Level C learning—that is, if the team extends outward to other subject-area teachers to inquire about

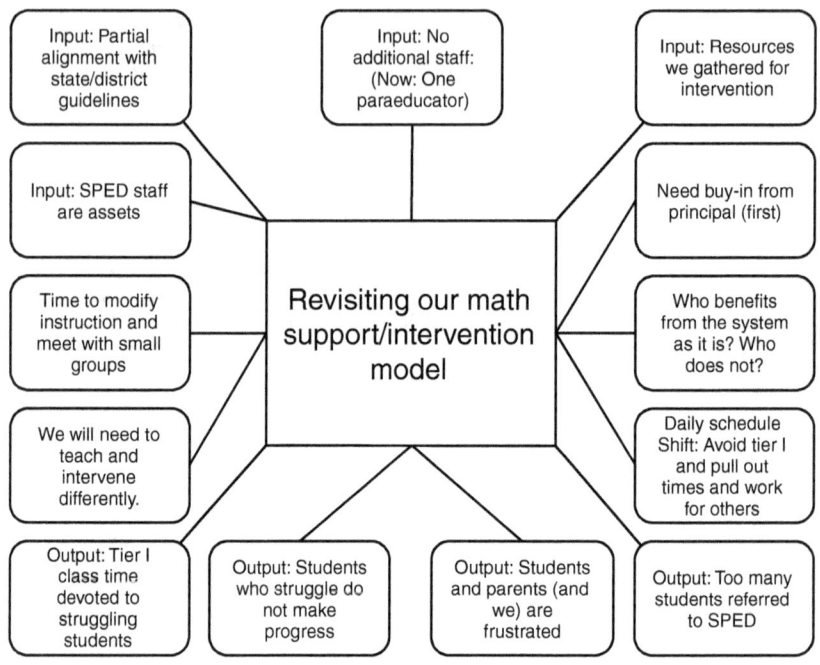

Figure 5.2 Sample free body diagram about math intervention system

their systems (Bryk et al., 2015). Heifetz et al. (2009) would likely label considerations of student success versus teacher recommendation and inter-teacher reliability in ratings as potential sources of productive disequilibrium if these data exposed challenges. The realization that school counselors provide students advice and recommendations with respect to student course selection recognizes the complex nature of this system (Shaked & Schechter, 2020) and emphasizes the need for a collaborative approach to address the challenge effectively (Heifetz et al., 2009), since any changes at the department level will be for naught if school counselors continue to advise students with the old set of guidelines. Recognizing that administrative approval might be needed is a nod to the structural and political frames of Bolman and Deal (2017).

To understand this tool a bit more concretely, please find another *Free Body Diagram for Systems Thinking Tool* completed for a different set of teachers' chosen focus in Figure 5.2.

In this situation, a grade-wide team of teachers at the elementary level is considering changes to their math intervention model. Their tool looks a bit "busier" than the original tool shared because the team needed to add more bubbles to represent all their thinking about this challenge. Note that input considerations are linked by lines to the top of the center box, output considerations to the bottom of the box, and other considerations to the middle. This tool could be extended outward from the center box, creating an infinitely expansive model, as needed, depending on the complexity of the challenge.

In this sample, there are ample connections to systems-thinking research evident in the team's representation. First, the team has examined considerations across the structural (schedules, standards), the human resource (SPED teachers as assets, one paraeducator available), and the political (principal buy-in needed first) frames of Bolman and Deal (2017). The group appreciated that they had personal (that they will need to teach and intervene differently) and management (how to make it work in the schedule and going to special education teachers for assistance) concerns (Hall & Hord, 2019). They have made some anecdotal statements in the "output" bubbles about data that have pushed them into a productive disequilibrium (Heifetz et al., 2009). Finally, the group, though collaborating within a Level B learning situation, is hoping to branch out of their grade level to leverage Level C learning by tapping special education teachers' expertise about intervention and differentiation (Bryk et al., 2015). Ultimately, this tool could be used to help teacher teams examine their challenges and areas for focus more comprehensively before rushing to solutions.

Once a challenge or focus has been more clearly understood within its larger system, other tools can assist with moving toward solutions. I will share two tools here that can help teams examine challenges in a collaborative, methodical manner. The two tools each allow teams to unpack systems and offer improvements to address deficiencies they identify. However, the tools vary in their length and comprehensiveness. The first tool, the *System Improvement Tool*, which can be found in Table 5.2, is the more comprehensive model. This might be more useful for a large-scale change process and/or a complicated system, such as an intervention model for the entire school or a course-selection process at the high school level. This tool is aimed at Level C teams, where teacher leaders are among a larger team of educators at the school or district level. Note that an editable and printable version of the tool can be found in the Support Material collection for this book.

Table 5.2 System improvement tool

System Improvement Tool

Step 1: Naming the System

Think of a system in your school or district that you believe needs attention to improve its function. It need not be a complicated or even a named system. Please identify the system or name it here if it does not already have a name (e.g., early intervention, student discipline, MTSS, class selection, class placement, parent notification, end-of-day dismissal, SEL, etc.):

Step 2: Unpacking the System

Unpack the system to determine how it works (*or doesn't!*). This section is rather open-ended, but here are some systems-thinking questions (non-exhaustive list, of course!) to guide your analysis of this system. If a visual representation (i.e., model, flowchart, etc.) is helpful to you, create one.

- What is the purpose of this system?
- What is working well within this system? Not well?
- Who initiates this system's processes?
- Who is included in this system? Excluded?
- How do various roles participate in this system?
- How does this system work?
- What are the results from this system's work?
- What forum(s) exists for this system?
- What is the time line for this system?
- How are decisions made within this system?
- What permissions are required within this system?

Collaborative Professionalism for Teams' Work

How does information flow from this system to the wider staff?
How does this system interact with other systems in the school?
How do decisions in this system affect other systems?
What are root causes of challenges within this system?
Who benefits from and/or is harmed by this system?

Step 3: Identifying System Deficiencies and Possible Improvements
Based upon your unpacking of your system, identify deficiencies that can be addressed and propose realistic improvements to directly address the deficiencies. *Be as specific as you can* (e.g., communication breakdowns, insufficient role representation, absence of an appropriate discussion forum, absence of follow-up opportunities, absence of voices, unclear expectations, unrealistic or inefficient time line, lack of leadership, inadequate documentation, etc.).

Deficiency	Potential Improvements to Address Deficiency	Potential Effects (Intended and Unintended) of Improvements

Step 4: Building an Improved (*or Completely New!*) System
Recreate the unpacking of your system from Step 2. However, this time, include your potential improvements to your system. Again, if a visual representation is helpful, create one.

Step 5: Action Plan to Implement Improvements to Your System
Outline here what professional learning, communication, role changes, budgetary considerations, buy-in, coalitions, and so on are necessary to enact the changes to the system you have envisioned. A potential template sample is included.

Strategic Action Step	Resources Needed (materials, staff, time, etc.)	Time Line Start Date	End Date	Roles Involved	Evidence of Success

This table is a tool that educator teams can use to unpack systems in their schools, determine system deficiencies, and propose improvements to systems to address deficiencies.

The *System Improvement Tool* can be used as an organizer to outline a group's collaborative thinking about a problem of practice connected to a system. To provide a concrete example, as I did above with the *Free Body Diagram for Systems Thinking Tool*, I share a completed *System Improvement Tool* in Figure 5.3. The problem of practice I have used for this example is the disproportionate absence of student racial diversity in advanced coursework at a high school level. Thus, the system is named "Rigorous Coursework Process."

Collaborative Professionalism for Teams' Work

System Improvement Tool: *Sample*

Step 1: Naming the System

Think of a system in your school or district that you believe needs attention to improve its function. It need not be a complicated or even a named system. Please identify the system or name it here if it does not already have a name (e.g., early intervention, student discipline, MTSS, class selection, class placement, parent notification, end-of-day dismissal, SEL, etc.):

Rigorous Coursework Process

Step 2: Unpacking the System

Unpack the system to determine how it works (*or doesn't!*). This section is rather open-ended, but here are some systems-thinking questions (non-exhaustive list, of course!) to guide your analysis of this system. If a visual representation (i.e., model, flowchart, etc.) is helpful to you, create one.

What is the purpose of this system?

What is working well within this system? Not well?

Who initiates this system's processes?

Who is included in this system? Excluded?

How do various roles participate in this system?

How does this system work?

What are the results from this system's work?

What forum(s) exists for this system?

What is the time line for this system?

How are decisions made within this system?

What permissions are required within this system?

How does information flow from this system to the wider staff?

How does this system interact with other systems in the school?

How do decisions in this system affect other systems?

What are root causes of challenges within this system?

Who benefits from and/or is harmed by this system?

Teacher Leadership Practice in High-Performing Schools

Who benefits from the system?

predominantly, White and Asian students, who are placed in advanced coursework sections, and their families, who get what they are seeking for their children

Who does not benefit from the system?

predominantly, Black and Hispanic students, who are not placed in advanced coursework sections, and their families, as their children miss out on opportunities

How the system operates:

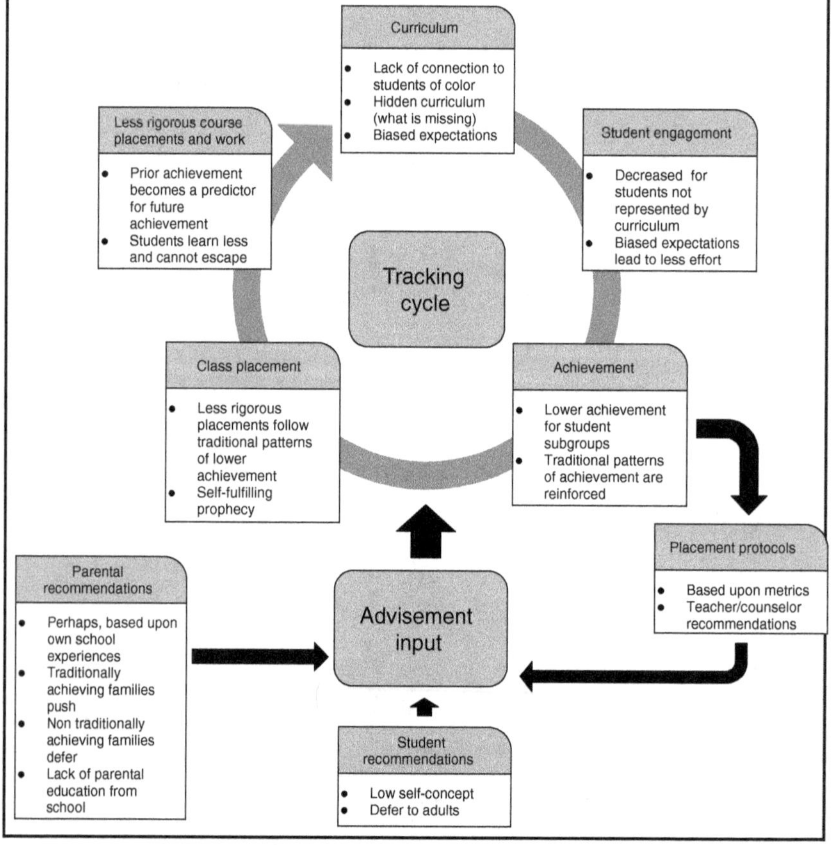

Tracking cycle

Curriculum
- Lack of connection to students of color
- Hidden curriculum (what is missing)
- Biased expectations

Student engagement
- Decreased for students not represented by curriculum
- Biased expectations lead to less effort

Achievement
- Lower achievement for student subgroups
- Traditional patterns of achievement are reinforced

Class placement
- Less rigorous placements follow traditional patterns of lower achievement
- Self-fulfilling prophecy

Less rigorous course placements and work
- Prior achievement becomes a predictor for future achievement
- Students learn less and cannot escape

Advisement input

Placement protocols
- Based upon metrics
- Teacher/counselor recommendations

Parental recommendations
- Perhaps, based upon own school experiences
- Traditionally achieving families push
- Non traditionally achieving families defer
- Lack of parental education from school

Student recommendations
- Low self-concept
- Defer to adults

Collaborative Professionalism for Teams' Work

Step 3: Identifying System Deficiencies and Possible Improvements

Based upon your unpacking of your system, identify deficiencies that can be addressed and propose realistic improvements to directly address the deficiencies. *Be as specific as you can* (e.g., communication breakdowns, insufficient role representation, absence of an appropriate discussion forum, absence of follow-up opportunities, absence of voices, unclear expectations, unrealistic or inefficient time line, lack of leadership, inadequate documentation, etc.).

Deficiency	Potential Improvements to Address Deficiency	Potential Effects (Intended and Unintended) of Improvements
disconnected curricula	revise curricula to be more representative of subgroups not represented in rigorous coursework	increased engagement increased achievement
insufficient marketing of rigorous course offerings	create informational material for parents that is easily accessible (i.e., website, screencasts, emails)	increased family awareness of and information about rigorous coursework
advising metrics that rely on results from cycle of tracking	revise metrics to be less dependent on prior achievement	students who have struggled in the past will not be continually punished
teacher encouragement of students focuses on high achievers	confer with all students to encourage them to register for rigorous courses	all students are encouraged to take rigorous courses
below-college track not aligned with rigorous coursework	eliminate below-college levels of coursework	all students can reasonably attain rigorous course placements
traditional beliefs about rigorous courses (parents, staff, students)	educate to build alliances supporting increased access to rigorous coursework for all	decreased resistance to changes

Step 4: Building an Improved (*or Completely New!*) System

Recreate the unpacking of your system from Step 2. However, this time, include your potential improvements to your system. Again, if a visual representation is helpful, create one.

Teacher Leadership Practice in High-Performing Schools

Who benefits from the system?

interested students from all backgrounds, who are placed in advanced coursework sections, and their families, who get what they are seeking for their children; all students, as the non-college-bound track of courses is eliminated

Who does not benefit from the system?

hopefully, no one

How the system operates:

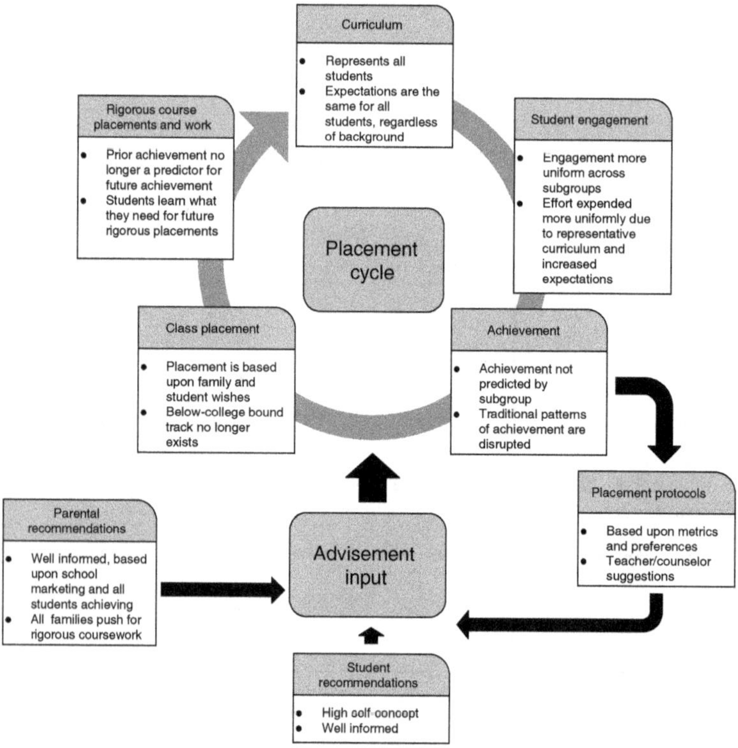

Curriculum
- Represents all students
- Expectations are the same for all students, regardless of background

Rigorous course placements and work
- Prior achievement no longer a predictor for future achievement
- Students learn what they need for future rigorous placements

Student engagement
- Engagement more uniform across subgroups
- Effort expended more uniformly due to representative curriculum and increased expectations

Placement cycle

Class placement
- Placement is based upon family and student wishes
- Below-college bound track no longer exists

Achievement
- Achievement not predicted by subgroup
- Traditional patterns of achievement are disrupted

Parental recommendations
- Well informed, based upon school marketing and all students achieving
- All families push for rigorous coursework

Advisement input

Placement protocols
- Based upon metrics and preferences
- Teacher/counselor suggestions

Student recommendations
- High self-concept
- Well informed

Step 5: Action Plan to Implement Improvements to Your System

Outline here what professional learning, communication, role changes, budgetary considerations, buy-in, coalitions, and so on are necessary to

Collaborative Professionalism for Teams' Work

enact the changes to the system you have envisioned. A potential template sample is included.

Strategic Action Step	Resources Needed (materials, staff, time, etc.)	Time Line		Roles Involved	Evidence of Success
		Start Date	End Date		
build allies for the changes to leveling and curriculum (form Rigorous Coursework Committee)	small group meetings (department, counseling staff, etc.), data about course enrollments, parental outreach (PTO meeting)	fall [year 1]	mid-year [year 1]	our team, principal, department chairs	coalition created; committee formed
present to board of education	data about course enrollments	spring [year 1]	spring [year 1]	members of committee; principal; department chairs	favorable response from Board of Education
curriculum revisions	samples of culturally relevant curricula; time	sum. [year 2]	sum. [year 2]	department chairs; curriculum supervisors; teachers	revised curricula that represent all students
professional learning on new curricula and goals of the Rigorous Coursework Committee	new curricular materials; professional learning time (i.e., faculty meetings, workshops, early-release days, etc.)	fall [year 2]	spring [year 2]	department chairs; curriculum supervisors; committee members	improved pedagogy, assessment, and results
marketing to families and students about rigorous coursework	website, robocalls, newsletters, screencasts	fall [year 2]	spring [year 2]	department chairs; curriculum supervisors; committee members	increased demand for rigorous coursework
eliminate non-college-bound leveled courses	course catalog	fall [year 3]	spring [year 3]	department chairs; curriculum supervisors; committee members	increased rigorous coursework for many students; increased diversity in rigorous courses

Figure 5.3 Sample system improvement tool about rigorous coursework process

This figure shows a completed sample of the System Improvement Tool in Table 5.2. This sample concerns how students can take rigorous coursework at the secondary level.

The selected challenge is a systems issue, indeed. It involves parents, students, teachers, counselors, administrators, and even the Board of Education. The tool provides ample room for expansion to include the complexity of the problem of practice. In this case, the system was seen as not working for families and students from traditionally marginalized backgrounds, while it worked just fine for White and Asian families, whose children were consistently filling the seats of the most advanced courses in the school. The team chose to create a visual representation of their system. Your use of the tool need not be so formal or electronically produced. The sample's visual representations were created by a computer program for readers' ease of understanding (and, I will admit, aesthetics—my handwritten versions were not nearly as attractive or easy to follow!). Practically, the team found a variety of systems-based deficiencies, not the least of which was a lack of information, both for helping a wide coalition of adults understand the problem to create urgency for change and allowing parents of all subgroups of students to make informed decisions about their children's class placements. Then, a new version of the system was envisioned, with deficiencies addressed. Finally, the team created a concrete action plan, spread over a three-year period, to implement their revisions to the system. Clearly, this action plan would require initiation, endorsement, and assistance from administrators, as these types of decisions are not typically left to teachers alone, so this situation represents the work of a Level C team. However, teachers are on the front lines, and they can recognize equity needs. With an increased understanding of the big picture and systems thinking, they are better equipped to help lead (or, at a minimum, support) change on such Level C teams.

For teams that are looking to make improvements to smaller-scale systems (e.g., collaboration on their own team, common planning for their lessons, parental communication at the team level, etc.), I share the *System Updates Tool*. You can find this tool in Table 5.3. Note that an editable and printable version of the tool can be found in the Support Material collection for this book.

Table 5.3 System updates tool

STEP 1: Describe your system. This is how _____ works in our [school/team/department].
(e.g., student intervention, course selection, student discipline, teacher collaboration, data-driven decision-making, master schedule development, etc.)
STEP 2: What works well in this system?
(i.e., communication, decision-making, representation, participation, results, messaging, timing, etc.) Note that it is likely that, given you chose this particular system for a gap analysis, there is not a lot to report here. However, it is important to find the pockets of success so you can build from them. Do not throw out what is working!
STEP 3: What needs improvement in our system?
(i.e., communication, decision-making, representation, participation, results, messaging, timing, etc.)
STEP 4: For each identified area in STEP 3, make concrete recommendations for improving the system and consider the intended and unintended effects of these recommendations.
(e.g., create a new communication channel, alter the leadership of the system, idealize the timing, provide for more participative decision-making, etc.). Consider the buy-in and coalitions that might be needed to enact these recommendations and note these in the final column.

Improvement Area	Recommendations	Potential Effects (Intended and Unintended) of Recommendations
Improvement Area 1:		
Improvement Area 2:		
Improvement Area 3:		

As with its more comprehensive cousin, the *System Updates Tool* is a means for teams of educators to gather their thinking about making improvements to a system they encounter. This tool might be more appropriate for a Level B group, such as a grade-level or departmental team. This tool can also expand to accommodate the level of detail and comprehensiveness a team desires. Though it is not as comprehensive as the *System Improvement Tool* (see Table 5.2 and Figure 5.3), the thoroughness of the team's analysis is limited only by time, the team's knowledge of the system, and its creativity for solutions. As with the *System Improvement Tool*, I will next share a completed sample so that the tool's use is more concrete. This sample can be found in Table 5.4.

Table 5.4 Sample system updates tool about common planning time

STEP 1: Describe your system. This is how Common Planning Time works for our team.
• We arrive within five minutes of the start of the time in the conference room. • We spend five to ten minutes making small talk and refreshing our memories on the work we completed the previous week. • We determine an area for focus (i.e., upcoming lesson or unit, based on data, etc.) and then begin to plan upcoming lessons. • We work in shared documents so we can all contribute in real time. • The team's members share resources, and one of us typically keeps a master copy of our work (anything that is not already in a shared document) to share with the group during or after the meeting.
STEP 2: What works well in this system?
• spirit of collaboration • creativity • work efficiency, once we settle on a focus • participation
STEP 3: What needs improvement in our system?
• efficiency upon arrival • determining a focus • transfer from one meeting to the next

STEP 4: For each identified area in STEP 3, make concrete recommendations for improving the system and consider the intended and unintended effects of these recommendations.		
Improvement Area	Recommendations	Potential Effects (Intended and Unintended) of Recommendations
Improvement Area 1: arrival efficiency	• leave each meeting with a focus for next week's work • document focus on a running log maintained by [member A]	• less wasted time/more collaboration time • work flows from one week to the next
Improvement Area 2: communication between meetings	• [member B] will send a reminder to the group about the upcoming meeting with: o the focus o what to bring	• all members have what they need • hit the ground running upon arrival • [member B] has work outside our meeting

In this sample, a grade-level or departmental team wishes to improve their work during common planning time. It seems that they already have a working system, but some improvements are needed so that their collaborative time is maximized. Their description of what is working well included excellent participation and even efficient work once they get going. However, the group recognizes that time is wasted in the transition between meetings, as they work to recall at the beginning of every meeting what they were undertaking in the previous meeting. Two rather simple adjustments to their communications system are recommended.

In the preceding section, the foci of big-picture and systems thinking were considered conceptually and practically via several tools teams of educators can use to examine problems of practice they face, with an eye toward making improvements. The final section in this chapter will allow you to reflect on your own school's collaboration.

Is Our School an Archipelago?

At the beginning of this chapter, I shared an analogy from geology—*the archipelago*—to illustrate the traditional isolation of teachers from one another in their practice. Given our learning in this chapter, it will be a valuable exercise to consider the degree to which your school manifests the type of collaborative culture I found in the studied NBRS. You will find a tool for this purpose, the *Is Our School an Archipelago? Questionnaire*, in Table 5.5. Note that an editable and printable version of the tool can be found in the Support Material collection for this book.

Table 5.5 Is our school an archipelago? Questionnaire

Is Our School an Archipelago?				
Directions: *Please rate each item on the following scale:* **never describes our school; sometimes describes our school; frequently describes our school; almost always or always describes our school; not sure.* For each item, respond with respect to the overall school (or grade level or department, if this is your level of analysis) culture, rather than your own individual practice. Note that the purpose of this tool is to generate conversation, not result in quantitative ratings.*				
1. Teachers in our school know what is happening in their colleagues' classrooms.				
never describes our school	sometimes describes our school	frequently describes our school	almost always or always describes our school	not sure
2. Teachers in our school are comfortable with colleagues observing in their classrooms.				
never describes our school	sometimes describes our school	frequently describes our school	almost always or always describes our school	not sure

Collaborative Professionalism for Teams' Work

3. Teachers in our school learn from each other regularly and in structured ways (e.g., peer observation, lesson study, teacher-led workshops, books studies, etc.).				
never describes our school	sometimes describes our school	frequently describes our school	almost always or always describes our school	not sure

4. Teachers in our school are *not* isolated from one another.				
never describes our school	sometimes describes our school	frequently describes our school	almost always or always describes our school	not sure

5. Teachers in our school work together to solve problems of practice.				
never describes our school	sometimes describes our school	frequently describes our school	almost always or always describes our school	not sure

6. Teachers in our school work together to plan instruction.				
never describes our school	sometimes describes our school	frequently describes our school	almost always or always describes our school	not sure

7. Teachers in our school have honest, and even difficult, conversations with each other, when needed.				
never describes our school	sometimes describes our school	frequently describes our school	almost always or always describes our school	not sure

8. Teachers in our school provide all students with a common experience across classrooms.				
never describes our school	sometimes describes our school	frequently describes our school	almost always or always describes our school	not sure

Copyright material from Jeremy D. Visone (2025), *Teacher Leadership Practice in High-Performing Schools*, Routledge

9. Teachers in our school take initiative and work autonomously to address challenges they recognize.					
never describes our school	sometimes describes our school	frequently describes our school	almost always or always describes our school	not sure

10. Teachers in our school understand how their work fits within the school's operation and purpose.					
never describes our school	sometimes describes our school	frequently describes our school	almost always or always describes our school	not sure

As with all tools shared in this book, this questionnaire is designed to generate conversation rather than produce numerical ratings. The ratings to select for each item are related to how much a given statement resembles the holistic status of teacher collaboration in the school (or department or team, depending on the unit of analysis), rather than one teacher's individual practice. Except for the choice "not sure," it is likely obvious to you that ratings selected farther to the right on the scale represent more collaborative (and desirable) characteristics, relative to the research I have presented in this chapter.

The discussion your team generates after answering this questionnaire could revolve around concrete examples of what individual items represent. For example, Item 3 asks about teachers learning from one another. There are a few examples provided in parentheses. However, if you responded this was "sometimes" or "frequently" your school's practice, what books clubs were offered by teachers? How was attendance at the book clubs? If teachers were facilitating professional learning workshops or other opportunities, was this the norm, or was teacher leadership in this area an outlier? What did peer observation look like? Again, how widespread was participation? These follow-up questions to any particular item will lead you and your school to develop plans moving you toward the types of collaborative practices evidenced in NBRS and outlined in the collaborative professionalism framework of Hargreaves and O'Connor (2018a) and this book. Only you and your team will know how your school aligns (or doesn't!)

with these collaborative practices and, with knowledge of your individual contexts, which practices might be best to address first. The good news is that you can address multiple items simultaneously, and in practice, as collaborative practices start to improve relative to one particular item, it stands to reason that they will improve in other areas as well, given their overlap.

Summary

This chapter began with a vignette of a highly functioning collaborative team—a middle school science team. This group worked effectively and efficiently with an administrator, the assistant principal, to recognize a common instructional challenge and problem solve as a team. Likely, this team would see a high degree of student success due to their strong collaborative practices.

The final key lesson from research on NBRS related to educator collaboration. These high-performing schools exhibited a collaborative ethos and systems for collaboration. The key lesson was articulated as: educators across roles, particularly teachers, do not work in isolation. Educators at our school learn, solve problems, plan, and innovate collaboratively.

With respect to the potential isolation of teachers, an analogy of the archipelago was introduced. Archipelagos are geological structures that feature a group or chain of islands that were created by similar geological events. Islands within an archipelago, while they might share some similar characteristics relative to their formation, relative age, isolation from the nearest continental landmass, and (if populated) their culture and language, also exhibit relatively unique features due to their physical isolation from each other. So, too, is this the case with many teachers' classrooms in a traditional educational model. At times, what happens in one classroom is completely unknown to the occupants of the next room.

The collaborative professionalism model (Hargreaves & O'Connor, 2018a, 2018b) was used as a lens through which the collaborative practices of NBRS were examined. The model has ten tenets, which include: collective autonomy, collective efficacy, collaborative inquiry, collective responsibility, collective initiative, mutual dialogue, joint work, common meaning and purpose, collaboration with students, and big-picture thinking for all. Within NBRS, many of these tenets of collaborative professionalism were noted in abundance. To start, these schools espoused a team and collective ethos that included replacing consideration for what was happening in individual classrooms with work for all students across the entire school. It was "we" not "I." Also, teams within these schools highlighted that they worked together to plan and solve problems of practice. Further, they learned with and from their peers in myriad ways, including peer observations, book studies, teacher-led workshops, lesson studies, and so on. Teacher leaders and principals in these schools noted that they found ways to overcome traditional walls of isolation.

With respect to the big-picture thinking tenet of collaborative professionalism, several frameworks about systems thinking were introduced, as these can be useful for teams to understand more completely and accurately the problems they face. The frames for system thinking presented included a four-frame model (Bolman & Deal, 2017), stages of concern (Hall & Hord, 2019), adaptive leadership (Heifetz et al., 2009), and levels of organizational learning in education (Bryk et al., 2015). These frames can help teams of educators, including their teacher leaders, to better "see" in systems, as they attempt to solve problems of practice within their own teams or contribute to leading more widespread changes on school- or districtwide teams.

The chapter provided multiple tools for educators to examine problems of practice. These tools included the *Free Body Diagram for Systems Thinking Tool*, *System Improvement Tool*, and *System Updates Tool*. These tools allow educators to use systems-thinking principles and prompts to understand the problems of practice they face more deeply, with an eye toward addressing deficiencies noted. To help readers understand the tools in a more concrete way, completed samples were provided for each tool.

Finally, the chapter concluded with a return to the archipelago analogy. A questionnaire was provided to generate conversation in schools about the strength of teacher collaboration. By using the questionnaire to examine the status of collaborative practice across a school, department, or team, educators can identify areas of strength and growth, so they can make concrete changes to address the areas for growth.

Questions to Consider for Chapter 5:

Collaborative Professionalism for Teams' Work

1. Consider the middle school science team in the chapter's opening vignette.
   a. If you are an administrator, how does this team's work align with teams at your school?
   b. If you are a teacher, how does this team's work align with teams at your school?
2. Consider the analogy of the archipelago.
   a. Is your school an archipelago?
   b. If so, in what ways does it align and not align with the analogy?
3. Given the various systems-thinking frames presented in this chapter, what resonated best with you, given your school's experiences?
4. Select a problem of practice to examine via the *Free Body Diagram for Systems Thinking Tool* (Figure 5.1) and complete the tool. What have you learned about this problem that your team had not considered before?
5. Based upon the scope of a problem of practice, select one of the systems-analysis tools (*System Improvement Tool* in Table 5.2 or *System Updates Tool* in Table 5.3) to complete. What are your next steps for addressing the deficiencies noted in the chosen tool?
6. Use the *Is Our School an Archipelago? Questionnaire* (Table 5.5) to generate conversation about teacher collaboration in your school, department, or team. Where will you start to improve teacher collaboration? (Note: if you did not find any areas for growth—*celebrate—together*, of course!)
7. Reflecting on your learning from this book overall, what have you learned about your school's practice?
   a. What practices/norms in your midst are affirmed?
   b. What practices/norms in your midst need improvement?
   c. What will you do about the areas for improvement?

Note

1 Pseudonym, as are all the names in this vignette.

References

Bolman, L. G., & Deal, T. E. (2017). *Reframing organizations: Artistry, choice and leadership* (6th ed.). Jossey-Bass.

Bräuchler, B. (2017). Changing patterns of mobility, citizenship and conflict in Indonesia. *Social Identities, 23*(4), 446–461. https://doi.org/10.1080/13504630.2017.1281468

Bryk, A. S., Gomez, L. M., Grunow, A., & LeMahieu, P. G. (2015). *Learning to improve: How America's schools can get better at getting better*. Harvard Education Press.

Elmore, R. F. (2000). *Building a new structure for school leadership*. www.shankerinstitute.org/resource/building-new-structure-school-leadership

Elmore, R. F. (2005). *School reform from the inside out: Policy, practice, and performance*. Harvard Education Press.

Goddard, R. D., Hoy, W. K., & Hoy, A. W. (2000). Collective teacher efficacy: Its meaning, measure, and impact on student achievement. *American Educational Research Journal, 37*(2), 479–507.

Hall, G. E., & Hord, S. M. (2019). *Implementing change: Patterns, principles, and potholes* (5th ed.). Pearson.

Hargreaves, A., & Fullan, M. (2012). *Professional capital: Transforming teaching in every school*. Teachers College Press.

Hargreaves, A., & O'Connor, M. T. (2018a). *Collaborative professionalism: When teaching together means learning for all*. Corwin.

Hargreaves, A., & O'Connor, M. T. (2018b). Solidarity with solidity: The case for collaborative professionalism. *Phi Delta Kappan, 100*(1), 20–24. https://doi.org/10.1177/0031721718797116

Hattie, J., & Anderman, E. M. (2019). *Visible learning guide to student achievement: Schools edition*. Routledge.

Heifetz, R., Grashow, A., & Linsky, M. (2009). *The practice of adaptive leadership: Tools and tactics for changing your organization and the world*. Harvard Business Press.

Mather, B. R., & Visone, J. D. (2024a). Peer observation to foster collective teacher efficacy: Teachers' perceptions about collegial visits. *Journal of Professional Capital and Community*, *9*(2), 85–104. https://doi.org/10.1108/JPCC-08-2023-0057

Mather, B. R., & Visone, J. D. (2024b). Peer observation to foster teacher self-efficacy. *Journal of Educational Research & Practice*, *14*(1), 1–22. https://doi.org/10.5590/JERAP.2024.14.1.01

National Oceanic and Atmospheric Administration. (n.d.). *How did the Hawaiian Islands form?* Retrieved February 25, 2024, from https://oceanservice.noaa.gov/facts/hawaii.html

Ross, J. A. (2013). Teacher efficacy. In J. Hattie & E. M. Anderman (Eds.), *International guide to student achievement* (pp. 266–267). Routledge.

Shaked, H., & Schechter, C. (2020). Systems thinking leadership: New explorations for school improvement. *Management in Education*, *34*(3), 107–114. https://doi.org/10.1177/0892020620907327

Shaw, K. L., & Gillespie, R. G. (2016). Comparative phylogeography of oceanic archipelagos: Hotspots for inferences of evolutionary process. *Proceedings of the National Academy of Sciences*, *113*(29), 7986–7993. https://doi.org/10.2307/26470854

Tschannen-Moran, M., Hoy, A. W., & Hoy, W. K. (1998). Teacher efficacy: Its meaning and measure. *Review of Educational Research*, *68*, 202–248. https://journals-sagepub-com.ccsu.idm.oclc.org/doi/pdf/10.3102/00346543068002202

Visone, J. D. (2016). A learning community of colleagues enhancing practice. *Kappa Delta Pi Record*, *52*(2), 66–70. https://doi.org/10.1080/00228958.2016.1156511

Visone, J. D. (2018). Developing social and decisional capital in US National Blue Ribbon Schools. *Improving Schools*, *21*(2), 158–172. https://doi.org/10.1177/1365480218755171

Visone, J. D. (2022a). Collaborative professionalism in US National Blue Ribbon Schools. *International Journal of Leadership in Education*, 1–22. https://doi.org/10.1080/13603124.2022.2107240

Visone, J. D. (2022b). What teachers never have time to do: Peer observation as professional learning. *Professional Development in Education*, *48*(2), 203–217. https://doi.org/10.1080/19415257.2019.1694054

Vygotsky, L. S. (1978). *Mind in society*. Harvard University Press.

Glossary

affective commitment a measure of how emotionally attached employees are to their workplaces

archipelago geological feature consisting of a chain of islands that are often formed by similar circumstances

collaborative professionalism model of effective educator interdependence outlined by Hargreaves and O'Connor (2018) characterized by 10 tenets: collective autonomy, collective efficacy, collaborative inquiry, collective responsibility, collective initiative, mutual dialogue, joint work, common meaning and purpose, collaborating with students, and big-picture thinking for all

collective autonomy condition in a school where teachers have more independence from formal, top-down authority and less independence from their colleagues, as identified by Hargreaves and O'Connor (2018)

collective ownership condition in a school where responsibility for educating students belongs to all educators in a particular unit of analysis (e.g., team, grade level, department, school, etc.)

collective teacher efficacy belief of a group of educators that they can collectively positively affect student outcomes, as defined by Goddard et al. (2000)

collegial visit specific format for peer observation characterized by a teacher-selected observation focus; full-lesson observation; and debriefing session that features all observation participants, including the host teacher

connected autonomy condition in a school where groups of educators leverage their collective learning to improve their autonomous work, as identified by Fullan (2019)

decisional capital ability for teachers to use what they have learned on their own and with the help of their colleagues to make the best decisions for students, as defined by Hargreaves and Fullan (2012)

five facets of trust a framework for examining trust among educators in schools; identified by Tschannen-Moran and Gareis (2015) as benevolence, honesty, openness, competence, and reliability

green light culture condition where leaders encourage innovation and new ideas, as identified by Kay and Boss (2022)

loose coupling challenge in U.S. schools noted by Elmore (2005) whereby teacher practice is insulated by administrative interference from outside scrutiny

math workshop model of mathematics instruction characterized by a routinized schedule of multiple learning modalities, including small-group instruction, individual conferencing, independent work, stations, etc.

National Blue Ribbon Schools schools recognized by the U.S. Department of Education due to nomination by their respective states and either overall or gap-closing student outcomes that rank in the top 15% of schools statewide in both English language arts and mathematics

Next Generation Science Standards set of national science standards released in 2011 characterized by three dimensions: cross-cutting concepts that transcend a particular scientific discipline, science and engineering practices, and disciplinary core ideas

peer observation modality of professional learning characterized by teachers learning via watching colleagues' instruction

Productive Zone of Disequilibrium principle of the adaptive leadership model of Heifetz et al. (2009) where leaders push others out of their comfort zone just enough to garner attention for the change and move change forward, but not so far as to cause irreparable damage and lasting harm to the organization

professional autonomy degree to which an employee has the ability to make decisions without oversight from formal leadership

shared governance condition where employees are provided more autonomy and decision-making capacity in their work

shared leadership condition in a school where leadership activity and authority are believed to be owned by many across the school in varying roles, including teachers

Glossary

social capital quality collaboration and professional relationships among teachers, as defined by Hargreaves and Fullan (2012)

Stages of Concern model for understanding the change process in schools, as developed by Hall and Hord (2019), which focuses on how individuals feel about changes

supported autonomy condition in schools characterized by a balance of ample support for teachers, through curricula, professional learning, administrative support, etc., and teacher autonomy of practice

Teacher Leader Model Standards set of standards for teacher leadership that outline leadership practices and ways that teachers can contribute; developed by an extensive consortium of educational organizations including public school districts, teacher unions, and higher education institutions, among other groups

teacher leadership leadership practice undertaken by educators who are not in formal leadership roles, including teachers, interventionists, related service personnel, paraeducators, social workers, school psychologists, etc.

teacher self-efficacy a teacher's belief that they can positively impact student outcomes, as defined by Tschannen-Moran et al. (1998)

tertiary education level of education beyond secondary (high) school; synonymous with a college education in this work

References

Elmore, R. F. (2005). *School reform from the inside out: Policy, practice, and performance*. Harvard Education Press.

Fullan, M. (2019). *Nuance: Why some leaders succeed and others fail*. Corwin.

Goddard, R. D., Hoy, W. K., & Hoy, A. W. (2000). Collective teacher efficacy: Its meaning, measure, and impact on student achievement. *American Educational Research Journal, 37*(2), 479–507.

Hall, G. E., & Hord, S. M. (2019). *Implementing change: Patterns, principles, and potholes* (5th ed.). Pearson.

Hargreaves, A., & Fullan, M. (2012). *Professional capital: Transforming teaching in every school*. Teachers College Press.

Hargreaves, A., & O'Connor, M. T. (2018). *Collaborative professionalism: When teaching together means learning for all*. Corwin.

Heifetz, R., Grashow, A., & Linsky, M. (2009). *The practice of adaptive leadership: Tools and tactics for changing your organization and the world*. Harvard Business Press.

Kay, K., & Boss, S. (2022). *Redefining student success: Building a new vision to transform leading, teaching, and learning*. Corwin.

Tschannen-Moran, M., & Gareis, C. (2015). Principals, trust, and cultivating vibrant schools. *Societies, 5*(2), 256–276. https://doi.org/10.3390/soc5020256

Tschannen-Moran, M., Hoy, A. W., & Hoy, W. K. (1998). Teacher efficacy: Its meaning and measure. *Review of Educational Research, 68*, 202–248. https://journals-sagepub-com.ccsu.idm.oclc.org/doi/pdf/10.3102/00346543068002202

For Product Safety Concerns and Information please contact our EU
representative GPSR@taylorandfrancis.com
Taylor & Francis Verlag GmbH, Kaufingerstraße 24, 80331 München, Germany

www.ingramcontent.com/pod-product-compliance
Lightning Source LLC
Chambersburg PA
CBHW052341230426
43664CB00041B/2603